RESOLVING
everyday
CONFLICT

RESOLVING
everyday
CONFLICT

Ken Sande
and Kevin Johnson

BakerBooks
a division of Baker Publishing Group
Grand Rapids, Michigan

© 2011 by Peacemaker Ministries

Published by Baker Books
A division of Baker Publishing Group
P.O. Box 6287, Grand Rapids, MI 49516-6287
www.bakerbooks.com

Updated edition published 2015
ISBN 978-0-8010-0568-8

Printed in the United States of America

The Library of Congress has cataloged the previous edition as follows:
Sande, Ken.
    Resolving everyday conflict / Ken Sande and Kevin Johnson.
      p. cm.
   ISBN 978-0-8010-1386-7 (pbk. : alk. paper)
    1. Conflict management—Religious aspects—Christianity. 2. Interpersonal relations—Religious aspects—Christianity. I. Johnson, Kevin (Kevin Walter) II. Title.
BV4597.53.C58S26   2011
248'.4—dc22   2011002289

17 18 19 20 21   7 6 5

CONTENTS

INTRODUCTION

Welcome!

Since you picked up this book, there's a good chance you're experiencing some conflict in your life. Welcome to the club!

Conflict is a normal part of life. As long as you live around other people, you're going to find your opinions and actions bumping up against someone else's. Sometimes you'll be able to simply back off and go your own way. But you have probably discovered that sometimes walking away doesn't work.

Many relationships are too important to walk away from. Some issues are too big to give in to. And some people just won't let go until they get everything they want. Add a variety of intense emotions to the mix, and conflict can get very messy and painful.

But it doesn't have to be that way. If you keep reading this book, you'll discover that conflict doesn't have to be painful or destructive. As you learn God's ways of resolving conflict, you can approach conflict as an opportunity to make relationships closer and stronger, to find solutions that are fair for everyone, and—best of all—to please and honor God.

Please and honor God? I'll bet that isn't the first thing you think of when conflict strikes. Well, it wasn't for me either. For the first twenty-five years of my life, my chief goal in conflict was to please and honor myself and get what I wanted. God was not in the picture. As a result, when I encountered conflict, I either walked over others or simply gave up on difficult relationships.

But while I was working as an engineer in the medical field, Jesus came into my life in a personal and powerful way. He began to change me in ways that turned my priorities upside down. He also gave me new insights and skills for dealing with difficult people. As a result, I became a more productive employee and was promoted. My friends told me I was a lot easier to be around!

God continued to transform me into a peacemaker during law school and my early days as an attorney. In one conflict after another—some of which had been tied up in court for years—God was working through me to bring peace in seemingly impossible situations.

I found peacemaking to be so rewarding that I became a full-time Christian conciliator in 1982. Since then I have been privileged to see how God's peacemaking principles can be used to stop divorces, rebuild marriages, restore friendships, reunite churches, settle lawsuits, and even bring peace between warring tribes in Africa and Asia. Seriously!

If you want to learn how to apply these principles in your life, keep reading this book. If you take these concepts seriously, your marriage, friendships, and job will never be the same. Instead of running away from conflict or being the one who always seems to make it worse, you can become the person others count on to bring understanding, justice, and reconciliation.

If you find the principles in this book helpful and want to dig deeper on specific peacemaking issues, read my book *The Peacemaker: A Biblical Guide to Resolving Personal Conflict,* which has been translated into eleven languages and is being used around the world to teach Christians how to resolve conflict. For more information on Peacemaker Ministries' resources, testimonies, training, or services, visit *www.Peacemaker.net.*

May God transform you more and more into a peacemaker and use you to bring peace into the lives of those around you.

Ken Sande

1

THE NATURE OF CONFLICT

What It Is and Where It Comes From

I travel often for work, and eating in restaurants can grow old. When I finally reach home, there's only one place I want to eat: our kitchen table. But while I'm away, Corlette's hands have been full managing our family, so when I get back, she loves to eat any place but home!

In the early days of our marriage, our differing desires on where to eat could lead to ridiculously intense conflict. When Corlette met me at the airport, I would hug the kids, kiss her cheek, and then quickly ask, "So what's for dinner?"

Sometimes she responded, "Ken, it's been a crazy day. I didn't have time to make anything. Can we just go out?" All too often my selfishness kicked in. With a deep sigh I replied, "Okay, if you really want to. But I wish you'd think of me once in a while. I've been on the road for days, all alone in drab hotel rooms, eating out three times a day. I'd just love a home-cooked meal."

"*Me* think about someone else?!" Corlette might reply. "You didn't even ask what kind of day I've had. The kids have been impossible. I had to take Mom to the doctor. And the dog threw up all over the carpet. But all you're thinking about is my pulling together a big meal for you!"

Sometimes one of us realized we were sliding down a slippery slope and saw it was time to turn the conversation in a different direction. Other times, I'm ashamed to say, we headed further downhill before we realized how selfish we were acting.

Never-Ending Conflict

Aren't you tired of all the fighting? From our homes to our neighborhoods, workplaces, schools, and churches, conflict surrounds us. As a lawyer and full-time Christian mediator, I have seen thousands of conflicts up close. I have witnessed divorce and custody battles, neighborhood feuds, personal injury actions, contract disputes, and church splits. As a former engineer and now as a ministry leader, I know how quickly a workplace can become poisoned by disagreements. As a husband and father, I understand the day-to-day frustrations families face at home.

Because I live in the same world you do, I know that chances are, you've experienced conflict recently as well. Perhaps you're experiencing the anguish of an unreconciled relationship right now.

I want to give you another way of handling conflict that you can use the rest of your life. Even though conflict is present in every part of life, I have seen peace come even to the most hopeless situations. I have watched people learn to work through the most severe differences, turning frustration into opportunity. They overcome division and enjoy harmony. Their anger gives way to love, mercy, forgiveness, strength, and wisdom. How do these amazing changes happen? Through a special kind of *peacemaking*. This peacemaking is applying the gospel and God's principles for problem solving to everyday life.

In the Bible, God gives us a powerful way to respond to conflict. Our natural approach to conflict is to focus on what an opponent did to us. Yet if we try to resolve conflict by focusing only on what someone else did wrong, we never reach a real solution.

God's approach begins with us understanding the gospel—everything Jesus Christ accomplished for us on the cross. Through the gospel, God treats us with extraordinary, unearned kindness. And his gracious response to us gives us power to respond to others in an entirely new way. Once we understand how the good news of Jesus empowers real reconciliation, we can begin to learn and apply God's practical steps to peacemaking. These steps aren't difficult to discover. They're clearly taught by Jesus and others in the Bible. God explains why conflicts happen and how we should deal with them.

Peacemaking is applying the gospel and God's principles for problem solving to everyday life.

Peacemaking comes naturally to no one. It always goes against our normal human impulses. But the more we draw on God's power, and the more we wrestle with and obey what God teaches, the more effectively we can work out disagreements with others.

What Is Conflict?

Conflict happens when you are at odds with another person over what you think, want, or do. Conflict can involve everything from small disagreements to major disputes, and it can result in not only hurt feelings, but also damaged property.

> **Conflict** happens when you are at odds with another person over what you think, want, or do.

Conflict begins when you don't get what you want. The conflicts you experience don't happen in a vacuum. They don't appear from nowhere. If you live in the Western world, you are most likely bombarded all day long by messages that are 100 percent about self. Life is all about me. My wants, my wishes, my desires, and my needs are much more important than anything you value. If you're a parent, you know that children absorb this message all day long. They hear, "I have the right to whatever I want. I have the right to have it my way. I deserve it." If this idea sinks in—the idea that I deserve whatever I want, whenever I want it—I'm going to get mad when I don't get it. And if I'm not getting what I want, I might start punishing others for it. That's where conflict starts. I fight because I'm not getting what I want. James 4:1–2 points out the source of conflict when it tells us, "What causes fights and quarrels among you? Don't they come from your desires that battle within you? You want something but don't get it. You kill and covet, but you cannot have what you want. You quarrel and fight."

Christians and Conflict

As Christians we can't escape conflict. Maybe you have picked up the idea that being a good person will help you steer clear of major clashes. If you try hard to do right, then people won't disrespect or mistreat you. Or perhaps you have been taught that if you do clash with others, turning to God for help will effortlessly make everything better. Life as a Christian doesn't work that way. We can't easily escape conflict, because we are all products of our own misguided desires. We are all part of the problem, and the problem is part of all of us. Even if we attempted to withdraw into a cozy cocoon, conflict would come with us.

Conflict happens among Christians because our sinful self gladly cooperates with messages that say "I can have whatever I want." We won't fight it because we like it. Our sinful nature never objects to the smallest outside encouragement to live for self. We find ourselves thinking "Yeah, it really is all about me. Maybe my needs are supreme. Maybe I should have what I want, and my needs are what I should be worrying about. I can't worry about what other people want. That's their problem." Like everyone else, we are prone to develop the total self-absorption that is the root of conflict.

Think and talk: Where are you seeing conflict in your life right now? What part does selfishness play in that dispute?

Unfortunately, conflict invades Christian relationships just as it does every other human relationship. Conflict happens among us in many ways. There might be loud disagreements, even public splits. Or there might be low-level conflict, behavior like gossip, slander, backbiting, criticism, undermining, etc. When our ministry staff asks churches if they experience conflict, they sometimes say, "Absolutely not. No conflict here." We ask, "Any gossip?" They say, "Lots of gossip." We ask, "How about backbiting?" They nod. Soon people start to get the point. People fight over worship styles, building design, curriculum, and everything else. Christians face conflict like everyone else. Even if we see our own brokenness and dysfunction, we don't know how to fix it.

Causes of Conflict

While many conflicts bring disastrous results, conflict isn't always bad. Even the most mature of Christians experience conflict and can come out better for it. In the New Testament account of the early Christian church, we read that conflict erupted because some people complained that they were being shortchanged in the distribution of food (Acts 6). The apostles responded promptly and wisely, calling a meeting to encourage discussion and develop a solution. The result was that the congregation selected seven trusted men to oversee the distribution of food. Verses 5 and 7 tell us, "This proposal pleased the whole group. . . . So the word of God spread. The number of disciples in Jerusalem increased rapidly, and a large number of priests became obedient to the faith." Conflict, handled well, became beneficial.

The Bible teaches that some conflicts come from God-given diversity. Each of us is like a different part of the human body, an analogy Paul uses in 1 Corinthians 12:12–31. We each have an important role to play; we each bring different perspectives and gifts to life. This God-given diversity leads to natural differences. Since God created us as unique individuals, we all have varying

opinions, convictions, desires, perspectives, and priorities. If we handle differences well, they stimulate dialogue, creativity, and change. They keep life interesting. Many of our differences aren't about right or wrong; they are simply the result of these God-designed personal preferences.

What God desires is unity, not uniformity. Instead of avoiding all conflicts or demanding that others always agree with us, we can celebrate the variety of God's creation and learn to accept and work with people who simply see things differently than we do. Unity means we are of one purpose, one mind, one heart. Uniformity means we are clones of each other, with everyone looking, thinking, and acting the same.

Other conflicts result from simple misunderstandings. There isn't a person on earth who communicates perfectly, whether speaking or listening. Countless conflicts arise when we think we have spoken and made ourselves clear—or we have listened and understood correctly—yet we jump to faulty conclusions. Our prejudices and impatience all feed our misunderstandings. Unfortunately, as fallen humans we tend to take offense and assume the worst. God wants us to assume the best until we actually know otherwise.

Although much conflict is the natural result of God-given diversity and simple misunderstandings, *many conflicts are the result of sinful attitudes and desires that lead to sinful words and actions.*

All of us say and do self-motivated, self-centered, sinful things—and those things all trigger conflict. Think again about James 4:1–2: "What causes fights and quarrels among you? Don't they come from your desires that battle within you? You want

something but don't get it. You kill and covet, but you cannot
have what you want. You quarrel and fight." This verse provides
crucial insights we will look at in greater detail in chapter 5. But
for now we should be aware of three important facts:

- People are different and want different things. *That's often the SPARK of conflict.*
- Differences get worse when sinful selfishness and pride drive our reactions. *That's the GASOLINE of conflict.*
- Destruction results when we fail to respond properly and allow our sinful desires to continue driving our words and actions. *That's the FIRE of conflict.*

The problem isn't where we start, but where we end up. The
issue isn't that we're different; it's what we do with our disagreements. Seldom do we choose to lay down our rights and
humbly work through our difficulties with others. Instead we
say, "We're different. I'm right. I've got to win."

spark
gasoline
fire

*We have natural differences—but our sinful nature is really
what makes conflict so destructive.* This is where the biblical
peacemaking process stands apart from almost all methods of
secular conflict resolution. While those methods talk about
resolving differences, they completely miss the sinful cravings
that are the gasoline that turns conflict explosive. Secular conflict resolution tells you that personal differences are something
you can simply talk through. It misses the biblical insight that

sinful desires often trigger differences that can only be resolved by a change of heart.

Our sinful desires fuel conflict in ways we probably haven't paused to understand. When we want something but can't get it, our unmet desire can work itself deeper and deeper into our hearts. Our desire becomes a demand, something we sin to obtain or sin if we can't obtain. Our hearts become controlled by our craving, ruled by something we want or love, something we serve or trust, something we depend on for comfort. What has actually happened is this: We have made the thing we desire into an object of worship. We have elevated our desire into a false god, what the Bible calls an idol. Not an idol of wood, stone, or metal, but a desire or craving that controls our lives.

The sinful root of conflict is really idolatry. As Christians, we know we should want what God wants, but when we allow an idol to control our hearts, we only want what *we* want. The one cure for idolatry is to look to God himself, returning him to his rightful first place in our lives and deciding we want his will for us above any other desire.

Think and talk: When in your life have you seen a desire grow into an idol?

The world around us doesn't help us put God at that rightful first place in our lives. Notice that while we are in conflict, the messages we hear pump on more and more gasoline. They echo back to us what our sinful nature is already saying: "You deserve it." "Stand up for yourself." "Don't get mad; get even." "Call 1-800-LAWYERS." It's tough to stand up to these messages. As people, our default mode is, "My needs reign supreme." Our sinful selves tell us we have the right to do what we want, and hardly anyone will tell us to look out for someone else. No one ever says to look out for number two; it's always, "Look out for number one." The resulting conflagration can set aflame every part of life, causing every kind of conflict and pain.

The Good News about Conflict

Jesus said that our response to conflict can prove we are his followers. Not long before his death, Jesus told his closest followers, "By this all men will know that you are my disciples, if you love one another" (John 13:35). Right before soldiers arrested Jesus and took him away to the cross, he prayed for believers in all times and places, pleading, "May they be brought to complete unity to let the world know that you sent me and have loved them even as you have loved me" (John 17:23). Jesus is predicting that the world will never know any real harmony apart from him. The world will be conflicted, just as we see it in homes, schools, offices, or neighborhoods. Yet our love as believers will prove to the world that we are Christians. Not only that, but our love for each other points to God himself. People who witness our love see his love.

The good news is that conflict doesn't need to ruin our lives. The grand theme of the Bible is reconciliation. We only have to read about four pages into the Bible—approximately five hundred words—before we see mankind leap into sin and experience separation from God and each other. Yet the whole of the rest of Scripture discloses God's incredible plan to bring back to himself a human race that willfully walked away from him.

The gospel is both vertical, bringing reconciliation between

God and human beings, and horizontal, bringing peace between individual people and groups. That's the amazing hope of the gospel. So there is no reason why Christians can't experience complete relational health with each other—and to the extent it depends on them, with non-Christians (Romans 12:18). We don't have to suffer with broken relationships. We don't have to live the way the world does.

Think and talk: How much hope do you have that God can empower you to resolve conflicts? Why do you have that expectation?

Overcoming Conflict

Unresolved conflict brings tragic results. When people lock horns at home or work, with friends, or in a courtroom, relationships are often severely damaged. Conflict robs us of time, energy, money, and opportunities. When we pause and realize the destructive nature of conflict, we discover how desirable peace really is.

Corlette and I found that our conflict over where to eat was a symptom of the selfish desires that sometimes ruled our hearts and spilled over into our marriage. As God convicted us of our sin, we confessed that we let selfish desires control our hearts, and we determined to find our complete fulfillment in him alone. We also asked God to reprogram our hearts so that we found more joy in pleasing him and serving the other person than we did in getting our own way. Little by little, God changed our hearts and gave us power to love in ways we thought were impossible. We are still on this journey of dying to ourselves, loving others, and practicing the peacemaking skills presented in the Bible, but with each step we are finding more delight in both God and each other.

Think and talk: What bad results have you seen from conflict? What good results could you enjoy by working toward peace?

Peace is worth our greatest effort. The Bible tells us that we should "make every effort to keep the unity of the Spirit through the bond of peace" (Ephesians 4:3). The Greek word in this verse that is translated "make every effort" means to strive eagerly . . . earnestly . . . diligently. It's a word that a trainer of gladiators might have used when he sent men to fight to the death in the Coliseum: "Make every effort to stay alive today!" Peace is worth that life-and-death effort. If we want to enter into all the peace God has for us, we have to give it our all.

As you learn God's design for true peacemaking throughout the rest of this book, may you find the peace we all so intensely desire.

2

THE HOPE OF THE GOSPEL

*Life-Changing Power that Can Heal
Your Relationships*

Wanting to give my family a little extra security, I called a locksmith to install a deadbolt on my front door. He sent a young apprentice to fit the lock while I was at work. When I came home, I was shocked at how poorly he had done his job. He had cut much more wood out of the door molding than necessary, and then only partially patched the hole with putty. It looked terrible!

I don't often lose my temper, but the shoddy workmanship really hit my perfectionist hot button. I drove to the lock shop. Inside I saw the locksmith behind the counter and two customers browsing merchandise. I had the locksmith cornered. If I confronted him in front of customers, he would want to look reasonable and not lose business. He would have no choice but to give in right away.

Talk about a stupid—and sinful—strategy. I walked up to the counter and announced loudly that his apprentice had "butchered my doorframe." Instead of trying to calm me down, the locksmith shoved back with defensive, angry words. The attorney in me rose to the occasion. Those poor bystanders witnessed a terrible verbal sparring match.

When my conscience finally kicked in, I realized I had dug myself into an embarrassing hole. I mumbled a parting shot and walked out the door, increasingly ashamed of what I had done. By the time I got to my car, I could clearly see my sin—about ten minutes too late—and knew I needed to confess my wrong and forgive him for his. But with a mountain of pride inside my heart, that seemed utterly impossible.

Radical Love for One Another

Despite the conflicts we encounter every day of life, the Bible lays out what feels like an impossible vision for relationships. Against the backdrop of sinful people tearing each other apart at every turn, Jesus said that Christians will stand out because of their radical love for each other. As we saw earlier, Jesus said, "By this all men will know that you are my disciples, if you love one another" (John 13:35). He prayed, "May they be brought to complete unity to let the world know that you sent me and have loved them even as you have loved me" (John 17:23). Our unity will even help reveal that Jesus is God (John 17:21).

Why is love so distinctive? Because the world doesn't know much about love. A world ruled by sin is a world ruled by self, so people never will experience real love apart from Christ. But

Christians have been changed by the gospel. Love, harmony, and unity are supposed to fill our lives. Unfortunately we often fall short, so many people identify us as Christians not by how we get along but by how divided we are. Whenever Christians fight—at home, in church, in any arena—everyone watches and thinks, "They're no different from the rest of us."

When Jesus lays out his vision of a life of peace, it might feel like he expects the impossible from us. There seems to be a chasm between the problem of conflict and his promise of peace. In a world that knows only fighting, how is peace possible?

The Gospel Makes Peace Possible

Just knowing the right thing to do never brings peace. We all know we *should* love. We all know we should lay down our rights. But it seems so far out of reach.

Our problem isn't knowing the right thing to do, but having the power to do it. We all know what it's like to make a resolution and fail to keep it. We pledge to try harder but fail. The same thing happens when we try to put God's commandments into action. His commands are faultless. The instructions of Scripture are uniquely helpful. But they don't contain the power to obey. As the apostle Paul explains, the law in itself is powerless (Romans 8:3). So all the relational tools and techniques in the world are meaningless without a power source. I could give you a list of ten surefire tips for being nice, but they could never make you a better person.

Just knowing the **right thing to do** never brings peace.

We have to admit that we can't in our own strength obey God's commands. As frustrating as that inability is, we have hope; God would never promise us love and healthy relationships if he didn't also give us the path to get there. God doesn't say, " 'By this all men will know that you are my disciples, if you love one another,' but you're never going to get there, because you're so evil." That's not the God we serve. He gives us the path. But we need to understand what it is. God has an answer to our inability to make peace. His answer is the gospel.

What Is the Gospel?

The gospel is God's power for peacemaking. And apart from understanding the gospel, we can't access God's power. The gospel is the incredible news that Jesus died on the cross to pay for our sins and rescue us from eternal separation from God, and that he rose from the dead to give us new life. Through faith in Jesus, we've been reconciled to God, adopted into his family, empowered to love even our enemies, and given the gift of enjoying him forever. Colossians 1:21–22 beautifully expresses the relational impact of the gospel: "Once you were alienated from God and were enemies in your minds because of your evil behavior. But now he has reconciled you by Christ's physical body through death to present you holy in his sight, without blemish and free from accusation." John 3:16 captures the simplicity of the gospel: "For God so loved the world that he gave his one and only Son, that whoever believes in him shall not perish but have eternal life."

Believing in Jesus means more than getting baptized, going to church, or trying to be a good person. None of these activities can erase the sins you have already committed and will continue to commit throughout your life. Believing in Jesus means, first, admitting that you are a sinner and acknowledging that there is no way you can earn God's approval by your works (Romans 3:20; Ephesians 2:8–9). Second, it means believing that Jesus paid the full penalty for your sins when he died on the cross (Isaiah 53:1–12; 1 Peter 2:24–25). Believing in Jesus basically means trusting that he traded records with you when he died on the cross—that is, he took your sinful record on himself and paid the penalty for that record in full, giving you his perfect record, which opens the way for peace with God.

This gospel gives us the gift of eternal life. But the gospel is more than a ticket to heaven. It isn't just for unbelievers. It's for every believer every day of life. But many Christians have a "two doors gospel." We think of the gospel as a door we enter at conversion. We stand outside of God's family, then someone shares the Good News with us, and the Holy Spirit opens our hearts to understand. We see our need. We trust in Christ. We come through the door into the kingdom of God. We believe, and the penalty of sin—eternal punishment—is taken away.

The gospel is more than a ticket to heaven.

But then—too often—we treat the gospel like an airplane ticket we save up to use on a distant day in the future. Having entered through one door, we put the gospel in our pocket until we come to another door. We don't pull out the gospel until we're in the hospital, facing only a few days to live. Then we peacefully tell our children, "Don't worry. I know I'm going to heaven because I trusted in Jesus. I believe the gospel and I have hope for eternal life."

Yes, the gospel provides great comfort when we face death. But there's a whole life we live between the first door and the second door. If we forget the gospel is for now—for sins we struggle with today, for areas where we still want to grow, for relationships that are broken—then we miss the rich treasure that belongs to us in Christ. There's a treasure stored up in heaven for us, but God doesn't want it reserved just for eternity. It spills into our daily lives today if we just reach up our hands and receive it.

The Transforming Power of the Gospel

We miss God's great plans for us if we think of the gospel only as the key to eternal life. God intends for the gospel to completely transform every area of our daily life. Yes, the gospel gives us eternal life. But it also makes us new creations with amazing new purposes and powers. The Bible promises us that God begins to make us new people in this life. Now. Today. Paul writes, "If anyone is in Christ, he is a new creation; the old has gone, the new has come!" (2 Corinthians 5:17). God gives us these new purposes and new powers for how we live in the next twenty-four hours. Again Paul writes, "He died for all, that those who live should no longer live for themselves but for him who died for them and was raised again" (2 Corinthians 5:15).

Those facts don't mean God is finished with me. Through the gospel I can confidently say God is remaking me. I'm not the person I used to be. I have a new purpose. Yet I wish that I began to act just like Jesus the moment I believed the gospel. I would prefer that all my sinful pride and selfishness and bitterness had gone away. But the real story is this: Through the gospel we enter a journey to become more like Christ. The

Lord continually works in our lives to change us into his image. Among other things, he constantly works in us to change how we deal with conflict.

God's approach begins with us understanding how graciously he treats us through the gospel of Jesus Christ. He shows us overwhelming kindness even when we don't deserve it. The gospel tells us everything God has done for us because of Jesus. The gospel informs us that we are new people because of him. And the gospel leads us into the implications for how we live today. You see this dynamic throughout Scripture, but it's taught so clearly in one of my favorite passages, Colossians 3:12–15. There we see how the gospel remakes our lifestyle and our relationships. As God's chosen people, we experience new life through the gospel:

> *Therefore, as God's chosen people, holy and dearly loved, clothe yourselves with compassion, kindness, humility, gentleness and patience. Bear with each other and forgive whatever grievances you may have against one another. Forgive as the Lord forgave you. And over all these virtues put on love, which binds them all together in perfect unity. Let the peace of Christ rule in your hearts, since as members of one body you were called to peace.*

When I read that passage, my natural inclination is to go right to the "shoulds." I immediately make a mental list of all the things I should be—compassionate, kind, humble, gentle, patient, and more. Then I try to live out those rules and find I can't do it. The commands are beyond my ability.

But there's an entirely different approach I can take. Instead of starting with what I should do for God, I start with what God has already done for me. I begin by discovering that I'm chosen by God and dearly loved. God has done all of that for me. And those gospel truths flow out into a different kind of life. They change me so I can become all those wonderful things. Because God bears with me, I can bear with others. Because he forgives me, I can forgive. Because he loves me, I can love and live in harmony with others.

God's Living Power

You might begin to grasp these gospel truths and think, "That still seems impossible." And you're right. You know you should love, but you can't. You know you should do this thing or that, but your willingness and desires aren't there. You need power. Understanding how kindly God treats us through the gospel of Jesus Christ is just the beginning of change. The gospel fuels peacemaking by inspiring and empowering us to seek after relational health we didn't think we could experience this side of heaven.

We also need to encounter the living power of the gospel, Christ living in us. Not just what God has done for us, but what he is now doing in us. Jesus wants to dwell in us so fully that both our mind and heart—both our understanding and our desires—are changed to be like his. The apostle Paul prayed that his friends the Ephesians would experience this kind of transforming power:

> *I pray that . . . Christ may dwell in your hearts through faith [so] that you, being rooted and established in love, may have power, together with all the saints, to grasp how*

> *wide and long and high and deep is the love of Christ, and*
> *to know this love that surpasses knowledge—that you*
> *may be filled to the measure of all the fullness of God.*
> *(Ephesians 3:16–19)*

"I know I should do this, but I just can't . . ." is the cry of every honest Christian. And in your own strength, you can't. But you can cry out, "God, I can't do this. I need your strength." You can pray, "God, I know I should forgive. But unless you do a work in my heart, I'm lost." You will find that God answers those prayers. He does a work of spiritual transformation in you. He softens and opens your heart, changing your desires. It's how you experience the living power of the gospel, Christ in you.

A Transformed Life

When God empowers you to treat others as he treats you, there's not a single part of your life that escapes the impact of the gospel. Here's just a glimpse:

- *You can love your enemies.* Even though you were his enemy, Jesus died to reconcile you to God. So you can imitate him by showing the same kind of undeserved compassion and sacrificial love to those who wrong you (1 John 3:16; Luke 6:27–28).

- *You can take initiative in resolving conflict.* You were still a sinner when Christ died for you. So you can make the first move to seek reconciliation with anyone who offends you or has something against you (Romans 5:8; Matthew 5:23–24, 18:15).

- *You can admit your own faults.* Because Jesus has already seen your sins in all their detail and taken them on himself, you can stop hiding your sins. You can bring your sins into the light through confession, trusting you will find mercy and cleansing through Christ (1 John 1:8–9).

- *You can make conflict an opportunity to witness.* Your life is no longer your own. Jesus bought you by his blood and made you a full-time ambassador of reconciliation. By his grace you can use every conflict as an opportunity to model his reconciling love and encourage others to believe in him (2 Corinthians 5:15–21).

Through the gospel, the Lord enables you to live out the principles of peacemaking in every moment of life.

Think and talk: How has the gospel changed your life?

The Power for Lasting Change

You might wonder if there's another way to experience real relational health. But every lasting change that takes place in our lives comes from what God does for us in the gospel. Author Tim Keller explains: "All change comes from deepening your understanding of the salvation of Christ and living out of the changes that understanding creates in your heart. Faith in the gospel restructures our motivations, our self-understanding, our identity, our view of the world."[1] The more we know and live in the gospel and all its implications, the more we will be transformed into Christlike peacemakers. There's a simple way to say this: "God saved me by giving his Son to die for me,

---

[1] Timothy Keller, *The Prodigal God* (New York: Dutton, 2008), 118.

proving that I am a loved, forgiven, reconciled child of God. Therefore I love, I forgive, I reconcile."

I am, therefore I do. Theologians make use of grammatical terms to summarize this principle. They say, "The indicative precedes the imperative." What God has done for me (the indicative) always comes before what I must do (the imperative). When I understand and experience what God has done for me, my response moves from "I should do that" to "I can do that," and ultimately to "I want to do that." If I understand how much I have in Christ, the result is glad obedience. If I really grasp and enjoy all the benefits of the gospel, the commands aren't a heavy list of rules. They are a joy.

The Gospel Changes . . . Me

That botched lock job reminded me why I need the gospel. Remember the locksmith I wronged? I stood in his parking lot for several minutes wrestling with my guilt. I knew I should go back in and admit I was wrong. But pride and shame paralyzed me.

So I began to pray. "Lord, I'm the biggest hypocrite in the world. I know what you want me to do, but I just can't go back in there. Please help me!"

God turned my thoughts to bigger things. He brought to mind the amazing graciousness of the gospel. God has already forgiven all of my sins—my countless sins—laying them on his own Son and giving me his spotless record. I'm forgiven in Christ! I don't need to wear a mask of self-righteousness. And I must not withhold from others the forgiveness God has lavished on me.

The more I prayed and thought about what Jesus has done for me, the more my heart was drained of pride and self-righteousness and filled with the desire and the ability to live out the gospel. When I went inside, my conversation with the locksmith couldn't have been more different from our first exchange. The gospel opened the way for me to confess how wrong I was. His heart quickly softened, and we were reconciled to each other. When he unexpectedly visited my church a week later, it was the gospel that allowed us to smile knowingly at each other and celebrate the forgiveness we have both received through Christ.

When we fully receive mercy from God, it can't help but flow out. That's how the gospel changes relationships. The gospel, when fully appreciated and embraced, overflows. It's God's power for peacemaking.

> The gospel, when fully appreciated and embraced, overflows. It is **God's power** for peacemaking.

3

ESCAPING, ATTACKING, OR PEACEMAKING

A Biblical Response to Conflict

Once, while teaching a seminar, I was approached by a woman, Diane, who told me about two engineers at her company. These top employees had a falling-out and refused to work together anymore. When they refused to collaborate on a high-priced consulting contract, the company president personally intervened for hours to convince the men to cooperate. After hitting a wall, he called in his Human Relations director, then an outside counselor. All efforts failed. Even the threat of being fired didn't end the standoff.

Diane told me she had recently completed a course on biblical peacemaking at her church, and she sensed God calling her to help the engineers. For several days she resisted the idea, but she ultimately felt compelled to approach the two men and offer to help them resolve their differences. She was surprised when they agreed, and that afternoon the three of them met in a vacant conference room.

At first both men were guarded and defensive, but as Diane prayed for guidance and slowly drew them out with thoughtful questions, the cause of their conflict finally emerged. A former supervisor had been envious of the two engineers' close working relationship and had lied to each man about the other to poison their trust. Because neither man went to the other to talk about the supervisor's statements, a canyon had opened between them.

When Diane helped each man realize how they had misjudged the other, the walls came down, opening the way for heartfelt confession and forgiveness. The next day they told the president they were ready to move ahead on the consulting project.

Diane recounted this story to me a year later. With a wide smile she told me, "When my co-workers heard what had happened, many of them approached me and asked for the 'secret' of my approach. I've had more opportunities to point people to Jesus in the last twelve months than I'd had in the last ten years!"

Conflict Is an Opportunity

Working toward peaceful solutions to conflict isn't our natural human response. Some people see conflict as a hazard that threatens to sweep them off their feet and leave them bruised and hurting, so they react by making every attempt to escape the situation. Others see conflict as an obstacle to be conquered quickly and completely, even if they hurt others in the process.

Yet there are others who have come to view conflict from a radically different perspective. *Peacemakers see conflict as an opportunity to solve problems in a way that not only benefits everyone involved but also honors God.* They use conflict to glorify God, serve others, and become more like Christ. They seize every chance to strengthen relationships, preserve valuable resources, and make their lives clear evidence of the love and power of Christ.

The Slippery Slope of Conflict

There are three basic ways people respond to conflict. We choose to escape, attack, or make peace. These responses can be arranged on a curve that resembles a hill, or a "Slippery Slope." On the left side of the hill we find escape responses to conflict. On the right side are attack responses. And in the center, on the top of the slope, we find peacemaking responses.

When conflict happens, the escaper focuses on running. The attacker aims at winning. The peacemaker's goal is reconciling—that is, restoring and repairing damaged relationships.

Imagine this hill is covered with ice. If you move too far to the left or the right, you lose your footing and slide down the slope. The farther you go to the side, the faster you slip downward. In the same way, an escape or attack response is likely to be followed by a more extreme response. That response usually makes matters even worse and leads to accelerated responses on both sides. And the more extreme your responses, the greater the damage everyone suffers.

Escape Responses

People use escape responses when they are more interested in avoiding a conflict than in resolving it. Some people believe all conflict is wrong or dangerous. They might think Christians should always agree, or they might fear that working through conflict does more harm than good and inevitably damages relationships. So these people usually do one of a couple things to get out of conflict.

One way to escape conflict is denial, pretending it doesn't exist. Or if we can't deny that a problem is real, we refuse to do what needs to be done to resolve a conflict properly. Good acting and broad smiles can fool many people, maybe even yourself. But people who are impossibly calm, agreeable, and sweet often aren't what they seem. In the end, denial brings only temporary relief and usually makes matters worse.

Another way to escape conflict is flight, or running away. Exiting a conflict completely is the response of many people. Besides quitting a job, flight tactics include leaving the house, ending a friendship, filing for divorce, or changing churches. Because running away delays finding a real solution to a problem, flight is almost always a harmful way to deal with conflict. Flight is sometimes appropriate as a way to respectfully and temporarily withdraw from a confusing or emotional situation—a pause to calm down, organize your thoughts, and pray. Flight is also a legitimate response to serious threats such as physical or sexual abuse. But deliberate time away from a situation needs to be followed up with every reasonable effort to find trustworthy assistance and seek a lasting solution to the problem.

Escape responses share some predictable characteristics. When I resort to escape responses, I'm generally focused on me. I'm looking for what is easy, convenient, or nonthreatening for myself. Using an escape response usually means I'm intent on *peacefaking*, trying to make things look good even when they aren't. Peacefaking happens when I care more about the appearance of peace than the reality of peace.

Escape responses are usually **peacefaking**, trying to make things look good even when they aren't.

Attack Responses

Plenty of people run from a fight. But not everyone. *People use attack responses when they are more interested in winning a conflict than in preserving a relationship.* Attack responses happen when people see conflict as a contest, or as a chance to assert their rights, control others, or take advantage of a situation. While attack responses are often employed by strong and self-confident people, they are also used by the weak, fearful, insecure, or vulnerable. Whatever the root cause, people use attack responses to apply pressure to eliminate opposition.

People move into the attack zone along one of two paths.

Some attack the instant they encounter conflict. Others move into this zone only after they try unsuccessfully to escape conflict. When they can no longer ignore, cover up, or run away from the problem, they go to the other extreme and attack those who oppose them.

The most common attack response is assault. Some people attack an opponent using physical force or by trying to damage a person financially or professionally. Others bully through manipulation and intimidation. Most frequent are verbal assaults, including insults and other vicious words, sometimes veiled in humor or sarcasm. Excusing yourself by saying "I didn't mean it" or "I was just joking" doesn't make words any less destructive. Whatever the form of assault, it always makes conflict worse.

Litigation is another attack response. Litigation isn't simply using the legal system to force a desired result. Even if we don't end up in court, we readily plead before the court of public opinion, going to family, friends, colleagues, and even strangers about our situation. We explain the harm we suffered. We build a case to sway them to our side. We continue the litigation in our own minds. We debate how we can win, replaying events and thinking, "I should have said . . ."

Actual courtroom litigation is a fact of life in business, schools, neighborhoods, and person-to-person issues. As often as people try to force others to bend to their will by taking them to court, *there are good reasons Christians are commanded to settle their differences within the church rather than in civil courts* (1 Corinthians 6:1–8). Civil litigation is one of the most brutal ways we can attack each other. It further injures relationships already gone bad, and when Christians are involved on both sides, their witness can be severely damaged. Lawsuits often fail to achieve complete justice. And while litigation might resolve a problem, it never achieves reconciliation. Can you see why it's vital to make every effort to settle a dispute out of court whenever possible?

Attack responses all share several characteristics. When I resort to an attack response, I'm generally focused on you, blaming you and expecting you to cave in and solve the problem. Attacks are *peacebreaking*, sacrificing people and peace to get what I want. Peacebreaking happens when I care less about our relationship than I do about winning.

> Attack responses are **peacebreaking**, sacrificing people and peace to get what we want.

Your Default Response to Conflict

The Slippery Slope is a powerful tool for spotting patterns in how we respond to conflict. When confronted with conflict, we all have a natural bent to either escape or attack. We tend to either run from a situation or stay and do battle.

My personal tendency is to flip between the two extremes. I'm inclined to ignore a problem as long as I can, but when I feel backed into a corner, I can come out swinging—a pattern of escape and attack. I am also a master at hit and run—a pattern of attack, then escape. By God's grace, I am learning to recognize these patterns and learn more constructive responses to conflict. With God's help, you can do the same thing.

> **Think and talk:** What is your usual response to conflict—escape or attack or both?

A Better Way

While our natural human reaction to conflict is to escape or attack, only peacemaking actually resolves conflicts. Escape or attack responses rarely resolve issues. If they seem to halt trouble, the relief is usually temporary. And whether we escape or attack, we usually say good-bye to part or all of a relationship. How many times has an escape or attack response alienated you from the people you love most?

I have found that when I energetically pursue *peacemaking* responses to conflict, I can expect a much greater likelihood of positive results. When I use a peacemaking response, I shift my focus from me or you to us. I watch out for everyone's interests in the dispute, especially God's, and I work toward mutual responsibility in solving a problem. Working toward peace makes it far more possible to achieve true justice and genuine harmony. It becomes far more probable that I will eventually reach reconciliation. Peacemaking is our best chance to keep conflict from spinning out of control.

Right now you have an opportunity to learn a better way of responding to conflict. Anyone can fake peace—or break peace. It takes no imagination at all to make a quick escape or launch a brutal attack when you find yourself in a painful conflict. But peacemaking truly offers you a new way to handle clashes of every kind.

If you want to stay on top of conflict—stay on top of the Slippery Slope—it's vital you consciously draw on God's resources. As we move into learning specific peacemaking tools, ask God to help you see your own natural impulse to escape or attack when faced with conflict. Ask him to help you acknowledge your need to learn better responses. Then, with a solid dependence on the gospel as the power for real reconciliation, you can learn and apply God's practical steps to peacemaking. You will discover real-life answers to the question, "How do I actually work this out?"

How do I actually **work this out?**

Peacemaking Responses

Peacemaking applies the gospel and God's principles for problem solving to everyday life. Practical peacemaking involves asking four important questions—four questions answered by principles we call the Four Gs. They are:

How can I focus on God in this situation?
G1: Go Higher.

How can I own my part of this conflict?
G2: Get Real.

How can I help others own their contribution to this conflict?
G3: Gently Engage.

How can I give forgiveness and help reach a
reasonable solution?
G4: Get Together.

In the midst of conflict it's easy to forget to do the right thing, and our sinful nature drags us to do the wrong thing. But the four questions alert us to the issues we need to work through in the thick of conflict—and the Four Gs teach us the practical things to do. These principles tell us who does what, who says what, and when. I have used these principles in hundreds of conflicts over the past three decades, and I have yet to encounter a situation in which they didn't provide practical and effective guidance. Whether I was facing a broken corporate system, a split church, a defiant teenager, or a marriage on the verge of collapse, the Four Gs have always pointed to a better way.

In the next chapters we will look at each of the Four Gs in detail. We start with the first G, "Glorify God"—learning to focus on God in our situation. In the middle of a conflict, God is usually the last thing on our mind. But he is the one who holds lasting solutions to our problems.

4

GI: GO HIGHER

Bringing God into Your Situation

I'm not an easy person to argue with. I often let pride rule my heart. I use my verbal skills to defend myself and make others look wrong. Worse yet, my training as an attorney has equipped me to use leading questions to back people into a corner.

No one has suffered more from these skills than my wife, Corlette. One morning she and I got into an argument over some trivial thing. After we traded a few jabs, she retreated to the bathroom to collect her thoughts and pray while I stood in the bedroom, planning like a prosecutor. I was just about to walk into the bathroom to lay out my case against her when the Lord brought a penetrating question to my mind: *How could I glorify God in this situation?*

I pushed the thought aside. I wasn't the least bit interested in glorifying God at that moment. My only concern was winning my case against my wife! But God pressed in with the same thought, this time in the form of a question I often use when mediating between people: "*How could* you *please and honor God in this situation?*"

The Holy Spirit took all the wind out of my sails. "Lord," I confessed, "please forgive my pride and self-righteousness. I know it won't honor or please you if I use my verbal skills to force Corlette to say I'm right. Please help me to admit where I've been wrong."

With a much different attitude, I went to her and said, "Corlette, I was so wrong to get defensive and blame you. Will you please forgive me?" Corlette had been expecting a full-bore attack. Now she was stunned by my words. Her face softened. She relaxed and replied, "No, it was really my fault. I shouldn't have approached you like that." Needless to say, the conversation only got better from there, as each of us put God's glory and the other's good ahead of proving ourselves right.

The Horizontal Problem

As this story shows, our tendency to ignore God in the midst of conflict creates an enormous obstacle to peace. When conflict heats up, God is usually the last thing on our minds. We're consumed with how the other person wronged us and how hurt we feel. All we think about is, "You did a bad thing," "You hurt me," "You deserve blame," "I need to get away from you," or "I need to crush you." I focus on me being right and you being wrong. I'm entirely horizontally focused, blind to everything but you and me and the problem between us. By looking only at the human issues, I leave God out of the situation.

As long as we leave God out of our situation, we can expect to stay stuck in conflict. It's as if we're stranded in a car on a lonely dark road without any power or know-how to get moving again. If we don't look to God in our conflict, we have to make do with our own limited resources. Instead of looking for God's help and creative insights, we remain locked into the options we can think of. Instead of noticing God's higher purpose of using conflict to demonstrate his love and power in our lives, we continue to see conflict either as a threat to flee from or a chance to force our will on others. We can't break out of our established patterns of escape or attack.

The solution to this "horizontal problem" is to stop and look up. Before conflict gets any hotter, we need to recognize God's presence and ask, "Where is God in this?" "What is God doing in this situation?" "What answers does he have for this conflict?" One of the most valuable things you can do in a conflict is to simply stop—just as you are about to say something to put conflict over the edge, just as you are about to cause relational wreckage, just as you are about to run away or fly into a rage. That's the time to simply STOP and ask yourself, "How can I please and honor God in this situation?"

How can I please and honor **God** in this situation?

Focus on God

The Bible gives us exceptionally clear direction on how to focus on God in the midst of conflict. The insight jumps out of a passage where the apostle Paul was writing to the Corinthian church. That small gathering of people was a mess. There was public fighting, morally inappropriate relationships, even drunkenness at church gatherings. The main problem in Corinth was that people were only looking out for themselves. They only cared about getting what *they* wanted. The Corinthian world brought a constant bombardment of messages like "Have it YOUR way" and "Do what YOU want."

Paul pointed out all the ways the Corinthians were striking examples of self-centeredness. Then he gave them a principle for focusing on God in every situation, including conflict. He wrote, "Whatever you do, do it all for the glory of God" (1 Corinthians 10:31). We call that principle the first G, for "Glorify God."

> "Whatever you do,
> do it all **for the glory of God.**"

Living for God's Glory

"Glory" is a Bible word for the essence of God. To live for "the glory of God" means you bring attention to, display, and reveal his greatness. When Paul urged the Corinthians to live for God's glory, he wasn't talking about an hour on Sunday morning. He wanted them to honor God and bring him glory in day-to-day life, especially in the way they resolved conflict.

You might never have thought about how your life can glorify God. *But when your relationships reflect his plan, you bring him glory.* When you draw on God's grace to put off your self-centered attitudes and act on his principles, you put his glory on display. Your life points to his vast wisdom, compassion, and transforming power. And as you live for God's glory, the impact reaches far beyond yourself, because you give everyone around you reason to respect and praise God. Glorifying God isn't about others seeing how great you are; it's about helping them see how great the Lord is.

What Are You Really Living For?

It's crucial to realize that you either glorify God or you glorify something or someone else. You're always making something look big. If you don't glorify God when you're involved in a conflict, you inevitably show that someone or something else rules your heart. If you don't focus on God, you unavoidably focus on yourself and your own will, or on other people and the threat of their wills. Put another way, your actions show either that you have a big God or that you have a big self and big problems.

Your best way to keep living for God is to continually ask yourself questions that bring your focus back to him. "How can I focus on God in this situation?" "How can I please and honor God in this situation?" "How can I bring praise to Jesus by showing that he has saved me and is changing me?" As I demonstrated in my conflict with Corlette, seeking to please and honor God is a powerful compass, especially when we face difficult challenges. Jesus himself was guided by these goals. He said, "I seek not to please myself but him who sent me" (John 5:30).

Three Ways You Can Glorify God

Conflict always provides an opportunity to glorify God. You glorify God—you show how big he is—every time you depend on his grace or all of his undeserved love, mercy, forgiveness, strength, and wisdom. But what does that look like in real life?

Let me offer three specific ways you can glorify God in the midst of conflict.

First, you can trust God. Our natural impulse is to rely on our own ideas and abilities as we respond to people who oppose us. But you can ask God to give you grace to depend on him and follow his ways, even if his ways are completely opposite to what you feel like doing (Proverbs 3:5–7). Above all, you can hold tightly to everything God has promised you in the gospel. If you trust that Jesus has forgiven your sins, then you can confess them freely to others. If you believe he uses the pressures of conflict to help you to grow, then you can cooperate with his work. If you count on his assurance that he always watches over you, you can quit fearing what others might do to you.

The question is this: Do you trust God enough to follow him wherever he leads you, even if the path looks difficult—or even impossible? You can only go forward when you realize that your powerful, loving God is on your side. As you seek to make peace, trust keeps you following God's path. Whatever you encounter, you can count on God's control and care. He never leads you into a situation not knowing what awaits you or how he will carry you through.

Do you trust God enough to follow him wherever he leads you, even if the path looks difficult?

Second, you can obey God. One of the most powerful ways to glorify God is by doing what he commands. Obeying God's commands without compromise honors him by showing that his ways are absolutely good, wise, and dependable. Our obedience also demonstrates that he is worthy of our deepest love and devotion. Jesus said, "If you love me, you will obey what I command" (John 14:15). If you want to honor Jesus and show that he is worthy to be loved more than anything in the world, learn his ways and obey his commands.

Nobody knows or keeps God's commands perfectly. But you can draw on God's power and grace to live up to what you know. And if you don't know how God wants you to think or act in a situation, dig into the Bible and ask more mature Christians for guidance.

Third, you can imitate God. When people in Ephesus were struggling with conflict, the apostle Paul gave them this timeless advice: "Be imitators of God, therefore, as dearly loved children and live a life of love, just as Christ loved us and gave himself up for us as a fragrant offering and sacrifice to God" (Ephesians 5:1–2). Imitating Jesus in the midst of conflict is the surest way to restore peace with those who oppose us. Whenever we live out the gospel in our lives and mirror Jesus' humility, mercy, forgiveness, and loving correction, we surprise the world and honor the Lord by showing his presence and power in our lives.

The Benefits of Glorifying God

Glorifying God brings him praise and honor by showing who he is, what he is like, and what he is doing in you. And glorifying God benefits you as well, especially in a conflict. Many disputes start or grow worse because one or both sides give in to their emotions and say or do things they later regret. When you focus on trusting, obeying, and imitating God, you will be less inclined to trip up in these ways. As Psalm 37:31 says, "The law of his God is in his heart; his feet do not slip."

Focusing on God is the key to resolving conflict constructively.

When you remember his mercy and draw on his strength, you see things more clearly. You respond to conflict more wisely, finding far better solutions to your problems. At the same time, you can show others that God truly exists and that he enjoys helping you do things you could never do on your own.

There's another benefit of a God-centered approach to conflict resolution. It makes you less dependent on results. Even if others refuse to respond positively to your efforts to make peace, you can find comfort in the knowledge that God is pleased with your obedience. That knowledge can help you to persevere in difficult situations.

Is This Worth Fighting Over?

Glorifying God opens up a surprising option. It gives you a choice to overlook an offense, showing the same patient mercy God shows you. You might assume that your commitment to making peace means you should immediately wade into a situation to work it out. If a boss reprimands you unfairly, you could instantaneously confront the mix-up. If a friend says something hurtful, you could straighten out your insensitive friend. Actually, that isn't always the best approach to peacemaking. In many situations, the best way to resolve a conflict is simply to let go of the wrongs others do to you. Instead of jumping in to address the wrongdoing, you can choose to overlook it.

Is this worth fighting over?

One great way to glorify God is by asking, "Is this worth fighting over?" Overlooking is highly recommended throughout Scripture. Look at these insights:

- "A man's wisdom gives him patience; it is to his glory to overlook an offense" (Proverbs 19:11).

- "Starting a quarrel is like breaching a dam; so drop the matter before a dispute breaks out" (Proverbs 17:14).

- "Above all, love each other deeply, because love covers over a multitude of sins" (1 Peter 4:8).

- "Be completely humble and gentle; be patient, bearing with one another in love" (Ephesians 4:2).

Those verses don't describe how most people act in everyday life. We don't often observe people dropping the matter . . . covering over . . . being patient . . . putting up with.

The ability to overlook a fault is rare. Yet that is how God treats us. He lavishes us with astonishing goodness and forgiveness. Psalm 103:8–10 reveals God's attitude toward us: "The Lord is compassionate and gracious, slow to anger, abounding in love. He will not always accuse, nor will he harbor his anger forever; he does not treat us as our sins deserve or repay us according to our iniquities." Go back and read each phrase of that passage again slowly. You can't help but see that God doesn't deal harshly with us when we sin. His kindness and patience toward us show us a fresh way we can relate to others.

Overlooking Isn't Giving Up

If you are by nature a peacefaker—pretending everything is okay when it's not—remember that overlooking isn't just another way to avoid conflict. And if you tend to be a peacebreaker—forcing your way on others regardless of how much you hurt them—realize that overlooking isn't a weak cop-out.

Overlooking is an active choice. Overlooking isn't

peacefaking—avoiding confrontation, staying silent for the moment but filing away the offense to use against someone later. That's actually a form of denial, which usually leads to a bitterness that eventually explodes in anger. When you overlook another person's faults, you deliberately decide not to brood over an offense. You stop replaying the situation in your mind. You quit talking about it. You choose to let it go. Overlooking means you choose to fully forgive a person without any further discussion or action.

Overlooking is a strong choice. Overlooking isn't peace-breaking—going through life battle-ready, on high alert. Yet overlooking is powered by all the strength of the gospel. Some people argue against overlooking by saying, "It isn't right to let people off easy." I have a quick answer to that. Whenever I hear a Christian speak those words, I ask, "Where would you spend eternity if God dealt us justice with no mercy?" The answer is obvious: We would all be condemned to hell. Fortunately, God doesn't treat us as our sins deserve. To those who have trusted in Christ, he is compassionate and merciful—and he expects us to treat one another the same way. As Jesus taught, "Be merciful, just as your Father is merciful" (Luke 6:36).

Overlooking is a practical choice. Overlooking is in sharp contrast to a life of constantly correcting others in the name of peace. Constantly correcting others likely causes damage, while overlooking helps relationships. Instead of calling each other to account for every fault, we can overlook smaller offenses. Doing this creates an atmosphere of grace, where we can let go of some hurts and move on with life.

Think and talk: When have you overlooked an offense and experienced a good result?

When You Should—and Shouldn't—Let It Go

Overlooking is a peacemaker's first option in responding to conflict, but it isn't your only option. It's the choice you can consider before you even begin to think of taking other steps to correct a situation. Yet overlooking clearly isn't the right choice when a wrong

- is damaging your relationship with a person;
- is hurting other people;
- is hurting the offender;
- is significantly dishonoring God.

Each conflict calls you to consider the appropriateness of over-looking. Sometimes you know right away that a single wrong action is far too big to overlook. Other times a fault goes on and on, becoming a pattern in another person's life. While the offense might not be large, the abrasive effect grinds at your relation-ship. As time passes, you realize you can't let the problem go any longer. Then you need to go to that person and work through your conflict, using the specific strategies you will learn in the next chapters of this book. And keep asking God for wisdom to know what to do.

In real life, overlooking resembles good driving. Even safe drivers make mistakes. They might not signal in time. They misjudge a situation and pull out in front of you. Or they cut you off because they don't see you in their blind spot. Those are all mistakes you can often work around. Overlooking means treating others the way you want to be treated, giving them the same grace-filled tolerance you wish others would give you. Overlooking works for minor hurts, the small bumps of everyday life. It isn't the right strategy for handling major wrongs.

What Comes Next?

If we pause and think objectively about the issues we face in life, we realize most of our conflicts simply aren't worth a fight. We're often quick to focus on what we think is the high price of overlooking, what it will cost us to let an offense go. But we should also count the enormous cost of not overlooking. Our determination to hang on to an issue can result in an enormous bill in wasted time, energy, and money—costs that are easy to miss when we are caught up in what seems at the moment to be an important battle. At first glance "letting it go" or "getting over it" can look like a bad way to resolve conflict. But as a peacemaker, overlooking is often your fastest and least costly route to peace. In every conflict we need to ask ourselves, "Is this really worth fighting over?" When the issues are big, the answer is yes. But when the issues are small, the answer should be no.

What if disputes are too significant to resolve through quietly and deliberately overlooking an offense? Then you need more strategies for pursuing peace. The first G, "Glorify God," undergirds every effort you make toward peace. When conflicts are too big to let go, the other three Gs of peacemaking give you additional, indispensible steps for pursuing harmony in every part of life.

5

G2: GET REAL

Owning Your Part of a Conflict

I once mediated a dispute where a homeowner claimed there were serious defects in the construction of his home. When the builder refused to admit any fault, the two men went to court. After nearly a year of expensive and fruitless litigation, they asked me to mediate their dispute.

During our first meeting, neither man would admit he had done anything wrong. Instead, they kept blaming each other and listing the other person's wrongs. At the end of the meeting, I asked each of them to go home and spend at least thirty minutes praying a simple request: "Lord, please open my eyes so I can see how I have contributed to this problem."

That night, God worked in the builder's heart. When we met again the following morning, there was a different look on his face. He asked to speak first, and I nodded for him to go ahead. He humbly itemized the construction defects, admitted that they were all his fault, and promised to move quickly to repair them.

The owner was so surprised by this confession that he didn't know what to say. After a pause, he said, "Actually, this isn't entirely your fault. If I hadn't been so obnoxious and self-righteous the first time I talked to you about my concerns, we probably could have resolved this on our own instead of spending the last year in court. This is more my fault than yours." Needless to say, this mediation moved quickly to a complete and mutually satisfactory resolution. God had done it again.

Have you ever noticed in a conflict where our focus naturally falls? It's on the other person and what that person did wrong. We maximize his or her sin and minimize our own. Yet as we work to resolve conflicts, the last place we want to look—at our own faults—is actually the first place to start. We won't begin to find peace until we ask ourselves a tough question: How can I own my part of this conflict?

How can I own **my part** of this conflict?

The Log and the Speck

In conflict we naturally focus on what the other person did to us. But that won't solve the problem. Jesus himself pointed out that attacking the faults of others isn't where our problem-solving efforts should start. In Matthew 7:3–5, he helps us answer the question "How can I own my part of this conflict?" with one of the most vivid images in the Bible:

Why do you look at the speck of sawdust in your brother's eye and pay no attention to the plank in your own eye? How can you say to your brother, "Let me take the speck out of your eye," when all the time there is a plank in your own eye? You hypocrite, first take the plank out of your own eye, and then you will see clearly to remove the speck from your brother's eye.

"First take the plank out of your own eye, and then you will see clearly to remove the speck from your brother's eye."

Jesus uses exaggeration to make a radical point. He pictures a person with a log jutting from his eye who is trying to dab a speck of sawdust out of another's eye. Blinded by his own large problem, the first man is a hypocrite for trying to correct someone else. He needs to take care of his own fault first, because the log in his eye distorts his view of the problem. As long as the log remains, he can never see clearly. This principle is the second G of peacemaking—"Get Real."

You might read Jesus' words and conclude you should never talk to others about their failings. A careful read of that passage shows, however, that it doesn't forbid loving correction of others' flaws. Instead, it warns us against correcting others too quickly or aiming criticism in the wrong direction. Before we talk to others about their faults, we need to make sure we have faced up to ours. Jesus teaches us to take care of the plank in our own eye, and then we can see clearly to get the speck out of someone else's. If we have dealt with *our* contribution to a conflict, then we can legitimately approach others about *theirs*.

Jesus doesn't mean that our own sins are necessarily bigger or worse than others'. But they are our responsibility; they are under our control. So our own sins are the first thing we need to examine and correct when we face conflict. As Christians, our primary focus needs to be on our own sin and not the sins of others. Even if I have decided to overlook an offense, it's still critical for me to do a "log hunt." So ask yourself, "Did I contribute to or provoke the offense?"

Owning Your Part of a Conflict

If we're quick to focus on the faults of others, how can we ever discover our own part of a conflict? We often find we have two kinds of faults. One has to do with our thoughts and feelings, the other with our outward actions. First, we might have an *overly sensitive attitude* that allows us to be offended too easily by others' behavior. While sensitivity is admirable in both men and women, some of us react far too quickly to any less-than-perfect treatment by others. We need to work through that and give others the same grace we expect for ourselves. Second, we may have contributed to the conflict through our own *sinful behavior*. What we have done or not done in a situation might have made a conflict worse.

Few of us have developed a habit of identifying and owning up to our wrongs. But there are helpful ways to start. You can ask God to help you see your sin. Pray the words of Psalm 139:23–24: "Search me, O God, and know my heart; test me and know my anxious thoughts. See if there is any offensive way in me, and lead me in the way everlasting." At first, praying those words might feel threatening. But the rest of this psalm powerfully reminds you that the God who sees you at your worst also loves you unconditionally.

You can study the Bible to discern where you fall short of God's expectations. Some Christians have no idea what God expects because they don't know the Bible. Hebrews 4:12 tells us that the Bible can help us to see ourselves more clearly: "For the word of God is alive and powerful. It is sharper than the sharpest two-edged sword, cutting between soul and spirit, between joint and marrow. It exposes our innermost thoughts and desires" (NLT). If you want to discover God's way to live in any area of life, the Bible is where you turn.

You can ask a spiritually mature friend to help you spot your failings. Proverbs 19:20 teaches, "Listen to advice and accept instruction, and in the end you will be wise." The older I get, the less I trust myself to be impartial about my contribution to a conflict. So I have surrounded myself with family, friends, co-workers, and other spiritual partners who can openly critique my role. I don't always like what these special people have to say, but when I humble myself and listen to their correction, they always help me see things more clearly. In particular, these friends can help me spot the idols I mentioned in chapter 1. An idol is anything I let control my heart. I make it a mini-god—it's something other than God that I depend on to make me happy, fulfilled, or secure.

Once we have begun to understand our part of a conflict, our job is to take real responsibility for what we have done wrong. Because most of us don't like to admit that we have sinned, we tend to conceal, deny, or rationalize our wrongs. If we can't completely cover up what we have done, we try to minimize our wrongdoing by saying that we simply made a "mistake" or an "error in judgment." If our sins are too obvious to ignore, we can still try to avoid responsibility by shifting the blame to others or saying that they made us act the way we did.

While we all love to point the finger at others, Jesus tells us to take responsibility for our wrongdoing. We have a statement we use at Peacemakers to encourage ourselves to own our part of the conflict. I find it helps me be accountable whether a fight is large or small, whether I started the conflict or just kept it going. Here it is: "Even if I'm only 2 percent responsible for a conflict, I'm 100 percent responsible for my 2 percent." As I work to resolve conflict, it really doesn't matter who did more. I need to take 100 percent responsibility for my piece of it.

If I'm only 2 percent responsible for a conflict, **I'm 100 percent responsible** for that 2 percent.

Taking responsibility for your part of a conflict is a crucial step toward peacemaking. But that honest admission isn't something you can keep to yourself. Once you admit to yourself that you did wrong, confessing your fault to the person you offended is how you fully own your part of a conflict.

Confessing your fault to the person you offended is the way you fully own **your part of a conflict.**

The Toxic Bad Confessions

There's a problem with most of our confessions. We naturally make weak and evasive apologies. Our sinful self-righteousness compels us to play down our faults, minimize our guilt, and make excuses for our wrongs. We see this tendency in politicians caught in infidelity, in athletes caught with steroids . . . and in ourselves whenever our wrongs come to light. Our bad apologies would be comical if they weren't so painful to the people we hurt.

Many people never learn to admit their wrongs honestly and absolutely. When you were a child, it was a good first step to learn to apologize. But as you matured you no doubt sensed the difference between a forced "I'm sorry" and a heartfelt "I did something wrong." Authentic confession means getting past cheap phrases like "I'm sorry if I hurt you," "Let's just forget it," "I guess it's not all your fault." Mumbling those feeble words rarely brings people back together.

These bad confessions are toxic. They do more harm than good. Suppose you say, "I'm sorry if I hurt you." What signal do you send with that little "if"? What does the other person hear? How does that person feel? You're really saying, "I'm not really convinced I did anything wrong," or "Deep down, I think this is more your fault than mine." Your confession might sound fine on the surface, but you're not sorry at all. You haven't taken any responsibility.

The Seven A's of a Good Confession

If you really want to make peace, ask God to help you humbly—and thoroughly—admit your wrongs. One way to do this is to use what we call the Seven A's. Not every confession needs all seven steps. In a minor offense, you can offer a fairly simple statement. The more major the offense, however, the better it is to do a thorough confession using all seven A's. As you endeavor to "get the log out" in any given situation, ponder which of these will be important.

1. *Address everyone involved.*

Real confession begins by admitting your sin to everyone directly impacted by it. Since every wrongdoing offends God, start your confession with him. Whether or not you admit a sin to other people depends on whether it was a "heart sin" or a "social sin." A heart sin takes place only in your thoughts and doesn't directly affect others, so it only needs to be confessed to God. A social sin involves other people. Confess those wrongs to anyone affected—a single individual or a group, and people you hurt or who just witnessed your wrongdoing.

The general rule? Your confession should reach as far as your offense. Suppose you were really angry with your spouse, and your kids were in the car and heard your angry outburst. You need to confess to your spouse, but you also need to talk to the kids.

2. *Avoid "if," "but," and "maybe."*

It's really difficult to find a confession that doesn't use "if," "but," or "maybe." It's so hard to give an unqualified apology! Yet the quickest way to wreck a confession is by using words that shift the blame to others or minimize or excuse your guilt. The classic bad confession is, "I'm sorry if I've done something to make you mad." The word "if" ruins the confession, because it implies that you don't know whether you did something wrong. It sounds like you just want someone off your back.

Notice how the following so-called confessions are diluted by the words in italics. "*Perhaps* I was wrong." "*Maybe* I could have tried harder." "*Possibly* I should have waited to hear your side of the story." "*I guess* I was wrong when I said those critical things about you." "I shouldn't have lost my temper, *but I was tired*." Each of these statements would have value if the italicized words were left out. These words neutralize the rest of the confession. They don't convey sincere repentance and won't soften the heart of someone who has been offended.

The word "but" is especially harmful, because it has the strange ability to cancel all the words that precede it: "I'm sorry I hurt your feelings, *but* you really upset me." "I should have kept my mouth closed, *but* she asked for it." "I know I was wrong, *but* so were you!" In those statements, most people sense that the speaker believes the words following the "but" more than those that precede it. Thus, a confession containing "but" rarely leads to reconciliation.

3. Admit specifically.

The more detail you provide when you confess, the more likely you are to get a positive reaction. Specific admissions help convince others that you are honestly facing up to what you have done, a signal that makes it far easier to forgive you. Not only that, but being specific helps you identify the actions, words, or attitudes you need to change.

For example, instead of saying, "I blew it as a friend," you could say, "I know I hurt you when I talked behind your back." Or instead of saying, "I know I'm not much of an employee," you might say, "I know I've had a very negative attitude the last few months. I've been critical of others and disrupted the operation of this office. It was especially wrong of me to criticize your work in front of others yesterday." As you strive to be specific in your confessions, make it a point to deal with your attitudes as well as actions.

4. Acknowledge the hurt.

If you want someone to respond positively to your confession, make it a point to acknowledge to him or her the hurt you caused. Aim to show that you understand how the other person felt as a result of your words or actions. "You must have felt really embarrassed when I said those things in front of everyone. I'm so sorry I did that to you." If you aren't sure how the other person felt, then ask. It can be dangerous to assume you know *how* or *how much* you hurt someone. You can say, "Have I understood how I've hurt you?"

5. Accept the consequences.

Accepting any penalty your actions deserve is another way to demonstrate genuine repentance. You might have to correct a piece of gossip you passed on. Or you might have to work extra to pay for damages you caused to someone's property. The harder you work to make restitution and repair any harm you have caused, the easier it is for others to trust your confession.

6. Alter your behavior.

You don't really mean that you are sorry if you don't commit to not repeating the sin. Sincere repentance includes explaining to the person you offended how you plan to change in the future by God's grace—what you will say, how you will act, or the attitude you will convey. Be specific. Find someone to hold you accountable. Explain that you are relying on God's help.

Sometimes it helps to put your plan in writing. It shows

you take the matter seriously and are willing to spend time planning how to change. Listing specific goals and objectives helps you remember your commitment. It provides a standard by which your progress can be measured. And your ongoing effort will continue to demonstrate your confession was genuine.

7. *Ask for forgiveness (and allow time).*

If you talk through each of those steps with someone you have offended, many will be willing to forgive you and move on. If the person you have confessed to doesn't express forgiveness, however, you can ask, "Will you please forgive me?" Your question signals that you are now awaiting their move. Don't be surprised if some people need time to forgive you. Reconciliation doesn't always happen right away, and pressure from you won't help.

If someone isn't ready to forgive you, make sure you have confessed thoroughly. If you sense that the person to whom you confessed is simply not ready to forgive you, it may be helpful to say something like this: "I know I hurt you, and I can understand why it might be hard to forgive me. I want us to be okay with each other, so I hope you can forgive me. In the meantime, I will pray for you and do my best to repair the damage I caused. With God's help, I will work to overcome my problem. If there's anything else I can do, please let me know."

Think and talk: Of the Seven A's, the "A" I struggle with the most is . . .

The Golden Result

As you work to remove the log from your own eye before you address the sins of others, you will discover that your honest admission of fault often leads to relationship breakthroughs. I call this the "Golden Result." The Golden Rule tells us to *do to others as we want them to do to us*. The Golden Result says that *people will usually treat us as we treat them*. If we blame others for a problem, they usually blame in return. If we say, "I was wrong," it's amazing how often the response will be, "It was my fault too."

I have seen this result in hundreds of cases over nearly thirty years of peacemaking, including the construction dispute I described at the beginning of this chapter. Whether the dispute involved a building project, a personal quarrel, a divorce, a lawsuit, or a church division, I've seen again and again that people generally treat one another as they are being treated. When one person attacks and accuses, so does the other. And once one person starts getting the log out of his or her own eye, it's rare that the other side fails to do the same. It's an exciting outcome of our efforts to put this principle into practice.

Keeping Confession Real

Proverbs 28:13 says that "He who conceals his sins does not prosper, but whoever confesses and renounces them finds mercy." Yet any time we use a process like the Seven A's, we are capable of turning it into a meaningless ritual and completely missing what God wants us to do. This usually happens when we use the process for our own benefit instead of seeing it as a means to glorify God and serve other people.

I have caught myself going through the Seven A's simply to

get a burden off my shoulders and minimize the consequences of my sin. In the process, I heaped even heavier burdens on the person I had already wronged. Since I had "fulfilled my duty," the other person felt coerced to forgive me, even though he sensed that my confession was insincere.

When you go to confess a wrong, remember that you are there to serve the other person, not to get comfort for yourself. Focus on showing God's love to the person you harmed. And regardless of that person's response, keep your commitment to repairing any damage you have caused and to changing your choices in the future. This is the fastest road to genuine peace and reconciliation. And once you get the log out of your own eye, you are better prepared to gently correct and restore others.

6

G3: GENTLY ENGAGE

Helping Others Own Their Part of a Conflict

Vickie was fired from her job for poor performance—and for a habit of making sniping comments about her employer, Julia. When she came to me for advice about her termination, Vickie was threatening to file a lawsuit for wrongful discharge. We spent a long time talking and praying about how she could please and honor God in the situation. As God worked in her heart, Vickie decided to go back to Julia and take responsibility for her contribution to the problem.

When the two women met the next day, Julia was expecting Vickie to ask for a financial settlement to avoid a lawsuit. Instead Vickie confessed her wrongs in detail, admitted that she deserved to be fired, and asked for forgiveness. Julia was so surprised that all she could do was mumble, "Uh, sure."

Vickie went on. "I appreciate your forgiveness." She paused, then continued, "I'd be happy to stop now. But if you would allow me to, I'd like to share a few things I have noticed where you may be contributing to the tensions with your staff. It might help avoid problems with employees in the future."

Vickie's offer was so sincere that Julia felt compelled to hear her out. Even though Vickie spoke respectfully, she noticed Julia's eyes begin to fill with tears.

Vickie paused. "I'm sorry," she said. "I guess I should stop."

"No, you don't understand," Julia replied. "You haven't hurt me. It's just that as you were talking, I realized that you're the first person I can remember who ever cared enough to talk to me like this."

With that encouragement, Vickie finished what she had planned to say, still speaking with respect. Although Julia didn't agree with all her observations, she was so grateful for Vickie's concern that she was able to receive her advice without offense. By God's grace, the two women parted in peace.

We've seen how the second G, "Get Real," says you shouldn't even begin talking to others about their sins until you have dealt with your own contribution to a conflict. If you do that first, your confession often encourages your opponent to admit fault. But not everyone responds so cooperatively. Some people take little or no responsibility for a problem, which puts you in an awkward position. Then if you bring up their faults, they might think your own confession was a sham. But if you walk away without bringing up their wrongdoing, they might never deal with their need for change.

Talking to other people about a conflict can be unpleasant. We unintentionally build tensions to the exploding point and then confront people with a list of their wrongs. The person we attack becomes defensive and shoots back with a list of our wrongs, which leads to a painful battle of words. Participants in the conflict who are verbally skilled may win arguments, but they will lose important relationships.

There has to be a better way to communicate with others about their failings. The time is right to ask, "How can I help others own their contribution to this conflict?"

An Opportunity to Restore

The Bible clearly says there are times when you need to address others' shortcomings. Having confessed your own contribution to a conflict, helping others own their part is often your next step in making peace. In his letter to the church in Galatia, the apostle Paul explains, "If someone is caught in a sin, you who are spiritual should restore him gently" (Galatians 6:1). This verse gives us the third G of peacemaking, "Gently Engage."

> "If someone is caught in a sin, you who are spiritual should **restore him gently**" (Galatians 6:1).

Encouragement to speak up to others about their sins appears frequently in Scripture. Jesus says, for example, "If your brother sins against you, go and show him his fault, just between the two of you" (Matthew 18:15). The apostle James writes, "Whoever turns a sinner from the error of his way will save him from death and cover over a multitude of sins" (James 5:20).

We have all met people eager to correct others—too eager!

Although the Bible endorses constructive correction, it doesn't give license to go hunting for faults to correct. In fact, anyone eager to go and show others their sin probably isn't the right person for the job. Being overeager is often a sign of emotional and spiritual immaturity, which cripples our ability to effectively help others. When Paul says to restore a sinner gently, he goes on to say, "But watch yourself, or you also may be tempted" (Galatians 6:1). We are at risk of falling into the same sins that afflict others. We might also be tempted to self-righteousness, pointing out sin in others as if we ourselves never fail. The best people to bring correction are usually those who prefer not to talk to others about sin but who do it out of obedience to God and concern for others.

Many of us feel reluctant to confront others' sin under any circumstances. We might fall back on Matthew 7:1, "Do not judge, or you too will be judged," concluding that the Bible forbids us to pass judgment on how others live. But we can be sure that Jesus isn't banning personal correction in that verse, because in the next breath he talks about the log and the speck, pointing out the necessity of admitting our part of a conflict before we address the role of others.

Some avoid correcting others by saying, "Who am I to tell someone else what to do?" While we don't have a right to force our personal opinions on others, we do have a responsibility to encourage fellow believers to be faithful to God's commands, living in ways that reflect the gospel, doing for others as God has done for us. Even with nonbelievers, we will sometimes have an opportunity to help those we love to live in ways that benefit them and the world around them. We can encourage peace in every part of life, among everyone we know.

We can better understand the urgent need to help others deal with sin by looking closely at Galatians 6:1. When Paul tells the Galatians to restore someone "caught in a sin," the Greek word translated as *caught* means to be overtaken or trapped. So the person who needs our help is one ensnared when caught off guard. He's like an inattentive fisherman who becomes tangled in his net as it's going overboard. He hangs desperately to the side of the boat, in danger of drowning. The fisherman and the person caught in sin have the same need—their problem has become so serious they might not be able to save themselves. They need someone to step in and help. Just as you wouldn't stand by and watch a fisherman drown, you shouldn't stand by and watch someone be destroyed by his sin.

Paul goes on to explain how to help the person caught in sin. We are to "restore him gently." That's the meaning of the word in Galatians 6:1 translated as *restore*. It means to "mend," "repair," "equip," or "complete." Each of these activities aims to make something or someone useful again. Our goal is to do good by mending broken people and restoring them to usefulness. That's a far cry from going to others with the intention of belittling them or doing them further harm. As pastor and martyr Dietrich Bonhoeffer wrote, "Nothing is so cruel as the tenderness that consigns another to his sin. Nothing can be more compassionate than the severe rebuke that calls a brother back from the path of sin."[2]

---

[2] Dietrich Bonhoeffer, *Life Together*, translated by John W. Doberstein (New York: Harper & Row, 1954), 107.

Those two insights can help you decide whether an offense is too serious to overlook—that is, whether you need to step in to help. First, keep the picture of being "caught" in mind. If a sin doesn't appear to be damaging relationships or doing someone serious harm, it might simply be best to overlook a sin and pray that God will show that person his need for change. On the other hand, if a sin appears to be dragging your friend under, don't delay in offering help. Second, remember the goal of "restore." Has a person's sin significantly hurt him and reduced his usefulness, like a large hole decreases the usefulness of a fishing net? If so, there may be a need for "mending," which can happen through a gracious conversation.

Going to another person to address sin can be one of the toughest things we ever do. It can call for enormous courage. But going might be the only means to rescue a friend and restore a broken relationship. As Jesus said, "If your brother sins against you, go and show him his fault. . . . If he listens to you, you have won your brother over" (Matthew 18:15).

Surprisingly, the Bible tells us to be the one who takes the initiative in going not only when others have wronged us, but also when we have wronged others—even when we *might* have wronged others.

When Someone Has Something Against You

When someone has something against you, God wants you to take the first step in seeking peace—even if you believe you haven't done anything wrong. If you think another person's complaints against you are unfounded or that a misunderstanding is entirely another person's fault, it's natural to conclude you have no responsibility to take the initiative in restoring peace. That's a false assumption. It's contrary to Jesus' specific teaching in Matthew 5:23–24: "Therefore, if you are offering your gift at the altar and there remember that your brother has something against you, leave your gift there in front of the altar. First go and be reconciled to your brother; then come and offer your gift." Notice that Jesus doesn't limit his command to situations where someone has something legitimate against you. Jesus said to be reconciled if someone has *something* against you, implying that an obligation exists whether or not you believe a complaint is valid.

If someone has something against you,
God wants you to take the first step in seeking peace.

There are several reasons you should initiate reconciliation even if you don't think you're at fault. Most important, Jesus commands you to go. You should also take the first step toward peace out of love for others and concern for their well-being. But there's a personal benefit in going first. You will have greater peace of mind by honestly facing any complaints others might have against you. By carefully listening to others, you can discover sins you're blind to—or have an opportunity to show others that their complaints are unfounded. Either way, you gain a clear conscience, an indispensable ingredient of real peace.

I recall one Sunday when I visited a small ranching community and preached a message on Matthew 5:21–24. After church, a friend took me out to lunch. Partway through our meal, a man I had seen in church that morning walked into the restaurant. Seeing me, he came over to our table, smiling with delight.

"I have to tell you what just happened!" he said. "Your sermon really shook me up, because I've got a neighbor who hasn't talked to me for two years. We had an argument about where to run a fence. When I wouldn't move it to where he thought it should be, he just turned his back on me and stomped away. Since I thought I was in the right, I've always figured it was up to him to make the first move at being friends again. This morning I saw that the Lord wants *me* to be the one to seek reconciliation, so right after church I drove over to his house to talk with him. I told him I was sorry for being so stubborn two years ago and that I wanted to be friends again. He just about fell over. He said he felt bad all along for stomping away that day, but he didn't know how to come talk with me. Man, was I glad I went to talk with him!"

When Someone Has Wronged You

God also wants you to go to others when you believe their sins are too serious to overlook. This is why Jesus said, "If your brother sins, rebuke him, and if he repents, forgive him" (Luke 17:3). It's sometimes difficult to decide whether another person's sin is serious enough that you need to go and talk about it. But here are a few simple tests that help me know whether it's time for me to go and compassionately show others their sin.

> God calls you to go and talk to others
> **if their sins are serious.**

I need to go when a conflict damages my relationship with someone.

You should go and talk about offenses that damage your relationship with another person. If you can't forgive an offense—that is, if your feelings, thoughts, words, or actions toward another person have been altered for more than a short period of time—the offense is probably too serious to overlook. Even minor wrongdoing can damage a relationship if it happens again and again. Although you might easily forgive something minor the first few times, frustration and resentment build if it continues to occur. Bring your concern to the other person's attention so the offensive pattern can be changed.

I need to go when a conflict is hurting others.

An offense or disagreement is too serious to leave unaddressed when it results in significant harm to you or others. The offender may be hurting you or others in a direct way. The person may also be setting an example that will encourage others to behave likewise. Knowing that "a little yeast works through the whole batch of dough," Paul commands us to address serious and open sin quickly and firmly to protect others from being led into sin (1 Corinthians 5:1–13).

I need to go when a conflict is hurting the offender.

Sin needs to be addressed when it seriously harms the offender—whether it's self-inflicted harm, like alcohol abuse, or harm to relationships with others or with God. Looking out for the well-being of others, especially family members or close friends, is a serious responsibility. Unfortunately, because many people take the view that everyone should be allowed to "do his own thing," many of us do nothing even when we see a loved one trapped in serious sin. That isn't the kind of love Jesus demonstrated.

I need to go when a conflict is significantly dishonoring God.

Sin is too serious to overlook if it brings significant dishonor to God. If someone who professes to be a Christian behaves in a way that others are likely to think less of God or the church or the Bible, it might be necessary to talk with that person and urge him to change his behavior. This doesn't mean we need to call attention to every minor offense, because God himself is patient with much of what we do wrong. But when someone's sin obviously affects how others see Christians as a whole, it needs to be addressed.

Go Person to Person on Your Own

Until now in this chapter I have emphasized when and why we need to "go and show" others their sin, because many of us are amazingly reluctant to go. It might take encouragement upon encouragement for us to do the necessary thing of going to others and helping them own their part of a conflict. But the Bible doesn't tell us simply to go. It also shows us *how* to go. As we have seen, our aim is to restore gently (Galatians 6:1).

Getting face to face is the best way to go to others. In Matthew 18 Jesus gives us a process for interacting with someone caught in sin, and it begins with going in person. I have already mentioned part of what Jesus says. In verse 15 he says, "If your brother sins against you, go and show him his fault, just between the two of you." Even before the arrival of all kinds of modern technologies, Jesus recognized that there is no substitute for talking to an opponent in person. As easy as it might be to make your point through a text, email, note, or phone call, a face-to-face conversation is still the best way to resolve conflict, because both of you can see facial expressions, read body language, and hear words. You will get your full message across and you will have the chance to clarify any misunderstandings.

Getting face to face is the best way to go to others.

Good listening is particularly important as you go. You can't assume you know everything going on, so don't point out someone's sin without giving them a chance to explain things. Making time and space to listen shows that you realize you don't have all the answers, and it tells others you value their thoughts and opinions. Even if you can't agree with everything you hear, your willingness to listen demonstrates respect and shows that you are trying to understand their perspective. Knowing that listening doesn't come easy for us, James gave this warning: "Know this, my beloved brothers [and sisters]: let every person be quick to hear, slow to speak, slow to anger" (James 1:19 ESV).

Before you go, carefully plan what you want to say. I rarely go into an important discussion without prepared notes to guide me. They give me a basic script to start the conversation, keep me on topic, and anticipate objections. When you need to talk with others about their faults, carefully planning your words can make the difference between peace and hostility.

Engaging others is more than simply confronting them with their wrongs. Many of us are hesitant to speak up about the sins of others. Of course, our caution might be a sign of peace-faking, pretending everything is okay when it's not. But once we decide to go, there is an equal and opposite danger. We often stomp into a situation with heavy boots. We lay into people for their sin. That's a sign of peacebreaking, caring more about getting our way and fixing a problem quickly than preserving a relationship.

If we want to be effective as peacemakers, we need to ask God to help us be discerning and flexible so that we can find the best approach to a given situation. Scripture rarely uses words we would translate as "confront" to describe the process of talking to others about their faults. Instead, it calls us to use a wide spectrum of activities to minister to others, including confessing, teaching, instructing, reasoning with, showing, encouraging, correcting, or warning. God wants us to adjust the intensity of our communication to fit the other person's position and the urgency of the situation. We are also warned not to let disagreements with others degenerate into arguing.

Going with Others

If you can resolve a dispute personally and privately, you should do so. But sometimes you need help to resolve conflict. If you draw on God's grace and follow the instructions he has given us in the Bible, you might be surprised how quickly and effectively you can resolve most conflicts on your own. But if going one-to-one doesn't resolve an issue, Jesus gives a next step. He says to involve others. "But if he will not listen, take one or two others along, so that 'every matter may be established by the testimony of two or three witnesses' " (Matthew 18:16).

If we aren't able to resolve our differences in private, we may need to ask one or more respected friends, co-workers, family members, church leaders, or other mature and unbiased individuals to help us be reconciled. The principle taught in Matthew 18 is that we should try to keep the circle of people involved in a conflict *as small as possible for as long as possible*.

The point of bringing "witnesses" isn't to gang up on an opponent. Their presence is meant to calm and clarify. Witnesses can ask questions, give advice, and bring a Christlike tone to the conversation. They can help all sides communicate more effectively and explore possible solutions. Serving as a witness doesn't require that a person actually saw the situation firsthand, though that might be the case. While witnesses have no authority to force a solution, they might prod you or your opponent to confess wrongdoing by pointing out any words or actions that haven't measured up to Scripture.

If going with others doesn't resolve a conflict, there are still options remaining. After Jesus said, "But if he will not listen, take one or two others along, so that 'every matter may be established by the testimony of two or three witnesses,' " he continued, "If he refuses to listen to them, tell it to the church; and if he refuses to listen even to the church, treat him as you would a pagan or a tax collector" (Matthew 18:16–17). While those verses give us a process of conflict resolution and discipline in the church, they also point to the fact that there are outside resources that can help you take the next step in resolving serious conflict. One of those resources is Peacemaker Ministries.[3] We offer both training and trained reconcilers to help you find fair and lasting solutions.

---

[3] *www.Peacemaker.net*

Recognize Your Limits

Whenever you try to show someone his fault, there are limits to what you can accomplish. You can raise concerns, suggest solutions, encourage reasonable thinking, and pray for the person, but only God can move others to change. Paul described this separation of roles in his second letter to Timothy 2:24–25: "And the Lord's servant must not quarrel; instead, he must be kind to everyone, able to teach, not resentful. Those who oppose him he must gently instruct, in the hope that God will grant them repentance leading them to a knowledge of the truth."

As I reflect on these instructions, I always draw a line between *instruct* and *in the hope.* This line reminds me that when I go to offer correction to others, my job is to gently instruct, but it's God's job, and his alone, to change the other person. The more I focus on my proper role and avoid the temptation to play the role of Holy Spirit (by repeating my words over and over and trying to coerce or manipulate others to change), the more often I see people listen, soften, and respond to God's gracious work in their lives.

7

G4: GET TOGETHER

Giving Forgiveness and Arriving at a
Reasonable Solution

I just can't get over Pam's adultery," Rick told me. "She says she's sorry and she's begged for forgiveness. I said I forgave her, but I can't forget what she did or be close to her again. It's a huge wall between us, and I can't get through it."

"I'm sure you're both in terrible pain," I said. "But I don't think divorce is going to end it. You'll just trade one kind of pain for another. There's a way to keep your marriage together and truly put the past behind you. But you won't find it with the empty kind of forgiveness you've offered Pam."

"What do you mean, 'empty kind of forgiveness'?"

"Rick, imagine you had just confessed a serious sin to God,

and for the first time in your life he spoke to you audibly: 'I forgive you, Rick, but I can't ever be close to you again.' How would you feel?"

His eyes widened. "I guess I'd feel like God hadn't really forgiven me."

"But isn't that exactly what you're doing with Pam?" I asked.

Rick looked at the floor, wrestling for an answer.

I continued, "Imagine instead that God said, 'Rick, I forgive you. I promise I will never think about your sin again. I promise to never bring it up and use it against you. I promise not to talk to others about it. And I promise not to let this sin stand between us or hinder our relationship.' "

After a long silence, tears began to fill Rick's eyes. "I would know I was completely forgiven."

As this story illustrates, there comes a point in a conflict when people know they should say words like "I'm sorry" and "I forgive you." But what do those phrases really mean? What do they accomplish? If the steps to forgiveness were obvious and if forgiving were easy, Christians wouldn't struggle with bitterness and unforgiveness. But offering forgiveness can feel impossible. It frequently raises complex issues. Yet as you press on in making peace, God will enable you to ask and answer the question "How can I truly forgive others and find reasonable solutions to the issues that divide us?"

Forgiven and Forgiving

Forgiveness is a powerful act that opens up the possibility of a relationship being fully healed from the pain of conflict.

Forgiveness is how you move from merely solving a problem to repairing your relationship. It's the means of finding lasting solutions and enduring peace. Giving and receiving true heart forgiveness is how we experience reconciliation, and Jesus instructs us not to settle for anything less. He said, "Therefore, if you are offering your gift at the altar and there remember that your brother has something against you, leave your gift there in front of the altar. First go and be reconciled to your brother, then come and offer your gift" (Matthew 5:23–24). When Jesus commanded us to "Go and be reconciled," he gave us the fourth G of peacemaking.

As Christians, we can't afford to overlook the direct relationship between God's forgiveness and our forgiveness. The Bible says, "Be kind and compassionate to one another, forgiving each other, just as in Christ God forgave you" (Ephesians 4:32) and "Forgive as the Lord forgave you" (Colossians 3:13). When it comes to granting forgiveness, God calls us to what feels like an outrageously high standard. Fortunately, he also gives us the grace and guidance we need to forgive others as he has forgiven us.

*Christians are the most **forgiven** people in the world. Therefore, we should be the most **forgiving** people in the world.* Most of us know from experience, however, that it's seldom easy to forgive others genuinely and completely, especially when we've been deeply hurt. We often find ourselves practicing a form of forgiveness that doesn't bring healing. Maybe you have said or thought the same thing Rick did about his wife: "I just can't be close to her again." Think of this statement in light of a prayer you likely have prayed many times: "Forgive us our debts, as we also have forgiven our debtors" (Matthew 6:12). We would feel great anguish if God forgave us with the kind of limited forgiveness we feel like giving others. Yet we can have hope, because forgiveness can become a reality in our relationships when we begin to understand what it isn't—and what it is.

What Forgiveness Isn't

To understand what forgiveness is, it helps to see what it isn't. First, forgiveness isn't a feeling. It's an act of the will. Forgiveness involves a series of decisions, the first of which is to admit that we are unable to forgive and ask God to change our hearts. As he gives us grace, we must then decide with our will not to think or talk about what someone has done to hurt us. God calls us to make these decisions regardless of how we feel. As you will see, however, these decisions can lead to remarkable changes in our feelings.

Second, forgiveness isn't forgetting. Forgetting is a passive process, letting a matter fade from memory merely with the passing of time. Forgiving is an active process involving a conscious choice and a deliberate course of action. To put it another way, when God says that he "remembers your sins no more" (Isaiah 43:25), he doesn't mean he *can't* remember our sins. Rather, he is promising he *won't* remember them. When he forgives us, he chooses not to mention, recount, or think about our sins ever again. Similarly, when we forgive, we must choose to draw on God's grace and consciously decide not to think or talk about what others have done to hurt us. This can require plenty of effort, especially when an offense is still fresh in our minds. Fortunately, when we decide to forgive someone and stop dwelling on an offense, painful memories usually begin to fade. Forgiveness isn't a matter of whether we forget, but of how we remember.

> ### Forgiveness isn't a matter of whether we forget, but of how we remember.

Finally, forgiveness isn't excusing. Excusing says, "That's okay," and implies, "What you did wasn't really wrong," or "You couldn't help it." Forgiveness is the opposite of excusing. Forgiveness says, "We both know that what you did was wrong. It was without excuse. But since God has forgiven me, I forgive you." Because forgiveness deals honestly with sin, it brings a freedom that no amount of excusing could ever hope to provide. The very fact that forgiveness is needed and granted indicates that what someone did was wrong and inexcusable.

What Forgiveness Is

Forgiveness is a radical decision not to hold an offense against the offender. It means to release a person from punishment or penalty. The Greek word most often translated as *forgive* means to "let go," "release," or "remit." It frequently refers to debts that have been paid or canceled in full. Another word for *forgive* means "to bestow favor freely or unconditionally"; it reinforces that forgiveness is undeserved and can't be earned.

As these words indicate, forgiveness can be costly. When someone sins, they create a debt someone has to pay. Most of this debt is owed to God. In his great mercy, he sent his Son to pay that debt on the cross for all who would trust in him. But if someone sins against you, part of their debt is also owed to you.

This leaves you with a choice. You can either *take* payments on the debt or you can *make* payments.

You take payments on a debt from others' sin in many ways. You might withhold forgiveness, dwell on a wrong, be cold and aloof, give up on the relationship, inflict emotional pain or gossip, lash back, or plot revenge against the one who hurt you. These actions might give you a moment of dark satisfaction, but in the long run they demand a high price from you. As someone once said, "Unforgiveness is the poison we drink, hoping others will die."

> **"Unforgiveness** is the poison we drink,
> hoping others will die."

Your other choice is to make payments on the other person's debt, releasing others from penalties they deserve to pay. Sometimes God empowers you to do this in one easy payment. You decide to forgive, and by God's grace the debt is swiftly and fully canceled in your heart and mind. But when you have been deeply wronged, the debt it creates can be too large to pay at once. You may need to bear the impact of the other person's sin over a long period of time. This might mean fighting against painful memories, speaking gracious words when you wish to say something hurtful, working to tear down walls and be vulnerable when you still feel little trust, or even enduring the consequences of an injury the other person is unable or unwilling to repair.

We don't have the means to make those payments out of our own human reserves. But Christ already has made them for us. While forgiveness can be extremely costly, if you believe in Jesus, you already have more than enough grace to cover the payments. By going to the cross, Jesus has already paid off the ultimate debt for sin. He's already established an account of abundant grace in your name. As you draw on that grace through faith day by day, you will find you have all that you need to make the payments of forgiveness for those who have wronged you.

God's grace is especially needed to release people from the ultimate penalty of sin—the pain of relational separation. It's the same penalty that God releases us from when he forgives. Isaiah 59:2 says, "But your iniquities have separated you from your God; your sins have hidden his face from you, so that he will not hear." When we repent of our sins and God forgives us, he releases us from the penalty of being separated from him forever. When we forgive others, we likewise release them from the penalty of personal separation. We don't let past sins cut off a friendship or keep us from building a future relationship.

Think and talk: When have you taken payments on a debt of sin owed to you? When have you instead made payments?

Two Components of Forgiveness

As we put forgiveness into practice, we discover it has two components—a heart component and a "transactional" or relational component. The heart component is releasing the offense to God. It's an attitude or disposition between you and God that doesn't depend on the other person's repentance. This component is wonderfully expressed by Puritan preacher Thomas Watson:

". . . when we strive against all thoughts of revenge; when we will not do our enemies mischief, but wish well to them, grieve at their calamities, pray for them, seek reconciliation with them, and show ourselves ready on all occasions to relieve them. This is gospel forgiving."[4]

Having an attitude of forgiveness is an unconditional commitment you make to God. By his grace, you work to maintain a loving and merciful attitude toward someone who has offended you. You choose not to dwell on the hurtful incident or seek vengeance or retribution in thought, word, or action. Instead, you pray for the other person and stand ready at any moment to extend forgiveness and enjoy reconciliation when the other person is ready to repent. This open attitude will protect you from bitterness and resentment even if the other person takes a long time to repent. While you wait for an offender to repent, you can keep these heart and transactional components in mind. Whether or not an offender has repented, you can always maintain a readiness to forgive. Once your opponent repents, you're ready to take the next step.

The transactional component of forgiveness happens between you and your offender. Unless you are dealing with a minor sin that can be overlooked, *granting* forgiveness is conditional on the repentance of the other person. Once that person confesses, you can extend forgiveness, releasing him or her from the offense and enjoying a fully restored relationship. Taking this step isn't appropriate until the offender has acknowledged wrongdoing. Until then, you may need to talk with the offender about his sin

---

[4] Thomas Watson in *Desiring God,* "As We Forgive Our Debtors," by John Piper, March 20, 1994, *www.desiringgod.org/resource-library/sermons/as-we-forgive-our-debtors*

or seek the involvement of others to resolve the matter. Once the other person repents, you can close the matter forever, the same way God forgives you.

Remember: An attitude of forgiveness is real. It isn't partial or "forgiveness lite." It's complete for you. As you obey Christ's command to offer forgiveness from the heart, to have an attitude of forgiveness, your burden lifts and your disposition changes. What isn't complete yet is reconciliation. Although being willing to forgive rests on you, reconciliation depends on both your willingness and the offender's repentance. But beware of one danger: Don't settle for an attitude of forgiveness just so you can move on. God always wants full reconciliation, so as far as it depends on you, keep reaching toward that goal. (See Romans 12:18.)

> Having an attitude of forgiveness rests on you, but **reconciliation** depends on both your willingness and the offender's repentance.

God vividly demonstrates both the heart component and transactional component of forgiveness. When Christ died on the cross, he maintained an attitude of love and mercy toward those who put him to death. He prayed, "Father, forgive them, for they do not know what they are doing" (Luke 23:34). After Jesus rose from the dead, the Father's answer to his prayer was revealed. Three thousand people heard the apostle Peter's first message and were cut to the heart when they realized they had crucified the Son of God. As they repented of their sin, forgiveness was completed, and they were fully reconciled to God (Acts 2:36–41). This is the pattern you should follow, "forgiving each other, just as in Christ God forgave you" (Ephesians 4:32).

The Four Promises of Forgiveness

When we forgive as the Lord forgives us, we release an offender from the penalty of being separated from us. We don't hold wrongs against others, we don't think about the wrongs, and we don't punish others for them. Therefore, forgiveness can be described as a decision to make four promises:

- "I promise I won't dwell on this incident."
- "I promise I won't bring up this incident and use it against you."
- "I promise I won't talk to others about this incident."
- "I promise I won't allow this incident to stand between us or hinder our personal relationship."

These four promises show us what forgiveness looks like in real life. Notice the first of the four promises is a heart component, and the other three comprise the transactional component. By making and keeping these promises, you make forgiveness practical. You tear down the walls that stand between you and your offender. You promise not to dwell on or brood over the problem, or punish by holding the person at a distance. You clear the way for your relationship to develop unhindered by memories of past wrongs. This is exactly what God does for us, and it is what he calls us to do for others.

Can You Ever Mention the Sin Again?

The four promises aren't meant to be used mechanically. As a human attempt to summarize the key elements of God's marvelous forgiveness for us, these promises make an enormously helpful peacemaking tool. But they are limited and imperfect.

In particular, the commitment to not bring up the offense shouldn't prevent you from dealing honestly with someone's recurring pattern of sin. For example, maybe you know someone prone to losing his temper. In the past he confessed his fault to you and you forgave him. Now he's verbally attacked you once again. Even though you're willing to forgive his latest outburst, you might believe he needs to get help for the issues that fuel his anger. If you point only to the most recent incident, he might shrug off your concern. You need to help him see he has an ongoing pattern of sin that requires real attention. By bringing up past offenses, you aren't breaking the second promise, because you aren't listing them off to use against him. You're instead bringing them up for his good.

Be careful, however, not to brush the second promise aside and automatically bring up others' past wrongs to bolster your case against them. When someone has confessed a wrong and you have forgiven him, you shouldn't bring it up again without a highly compelling reason. Otherwise you rob people of the hope that they can change or that you really mean to give them another chance. The more you deal with each situation as a fresh and unique opportunity to grow and to experience the grace of God, the more open others will be to listening to your concerns.

What About Consequences for Sin?

While forgiveness brings reconciliation to a relationship, it doesn't always release people from the real-world consequences of sin. When someone wrongs you, it takes wisdom to determine whether or not to enforce a set of consequences: Sometimes it's best to show mercy. But sometimes it's best to allow a person to experience consequences that teach a much-needed lesson. It all depends on what will most effectively glorify God and serve the other person. Think, for example, of a man who confesses to embezzling from a neighborhood organization. Can he be forgiven? Yes, but he shouldn't be the treasurer. A teen breaks a household rule for cell phone use and confesses it. Forgiven? Yes, but that young person might still lose phone privileges. Consequences can still exist even when forgiveness abounds. The essence of the fourth promise, "I promise I won't allow this incident to stand between us or hinder our personal relationship," is that you remove the consequence of a broken relationship.

Remove the consequence of a broken relationship.

You Can't Do It Alone

As you seek to live out the fourth G of peacemaking, "Get Together," remember above all else that true forgiveness depends on God's grace. In forgiving, you lay down your rights to justice, to money, or to something else that's valuable. So forgiveness costs you something. Forgiveness can cause real suffering. You can, however, ask yourself, "Where has the price already been paid?" It's been paid on the cross of Christ. If you try to forgive others on your own, you face a long and frustrating battle. If you continually remind yourself how much God has forgiven you and ask God to change your heart, he can enable you to offer forgiveness for even the most painful offenses.

We see a powerful display of God's grace in the life of Corrie ten Boom, who had been imprisoned with her family by the Nazis for giving aid to Jews early in World War II. Her elderly father and her beloved sister Betsie died as a result of the brutal treatment they received in prison. God sustained Corrie through her time in a concentration camp, and after the war she traveled throughout the world, testifying to God's love. Here is what she wrote about a remarkable encounter in Germany:

> It was at a church service in Munich that I saw him, the former S.S. man who had stood guard at the shower room door in the processing center at Ravensbrück. He was the first of our actual jailers that I had seen since that time. And suddenly it was all there—the roomful of mocking men, the heaps of clothing, Betsie's pain-blanched face.
>
> He came up to me as the church was emptying, beaming and bowing. "How grateful I am for your message, Fraulein," he said. "To think that, as you say, he has washed my sins away!"
>
> His hand was thrust out to shake mine. And I, who had preached so often to the people in Bloemendaal about the need to forgive, kept my hand at my side.
>
> Even as the angry, vengeful thoughts boiled through me, I saw the sin of them. Jesus Christ had died for this man; was I going to ask for more? "Lord Jesus," I prayed, "forgive me and help me to forgive him."
>
> I tried to smile, I struggled to raise my hand. I could not. I felt nothing, not the slightest spark of warmth or charity. And so again I breathed a silent prayer. "Jesus, I cannot forgive him. Give me Your forgiveness."
>
> As I took his hand the most incredible thing happened. From my shoulder along my arm and through my hand a current seemed to pass from me to him, while

into my heart sprang a love for this stranger that almost overwhelmed me.

So I discovered that it is not on our forgiveness any more than on our goodness that the world's healing hinges, but on him. When he tells us to love our enemies, he gives, along with the command, the love itself.[5]

When you realize that you can't ultimately forgive in your own strength—that only God can give you the desire and ability to truly forgive others' sins—then you will find the strength you need to give others the amazing gift of forgiveness and experience reconciled relationships.

[5]Corrie ten Boom, *The Hiding Place* (New York: Bantam, 1974), 238.

8

OVERCOME EVIL WITH GOOD

Pressing On with Deliberate Love

One day during my morning run I noticed a blind woman walking on the opposite side of the street with her Seeing Eye dog, a beautiful golden retriever. As I was about to pass them, I noticed a car blocking a driveway a few paces ahead of them. At that moment the dog paused and gently pressed his shoulder against the woman's leg, signaling her to turn aside so they could get around the car. I'm sure she normally followed his lead, but that day she didn't seem to trust him. She had probably walked this route many times before and knew this was not the normal place to make a turn. Whatever the cause, she wouldn't move to the side and instead gave him the signal to move ahead. He again pressed his shoulder against her leg, trying to guide her on a safe path. She angrily ordered him to go forward. When he again declined, her temper flared. I was surprised to see her suddenly kick him and order him ahead once more.

I was about to speak up when I sensed God wanted me to be silent and learn a lesson. Knowing he was likely to receive further abuse, the dog once more put his shoulder gently against her leg. Sure enough, she kicked him again, this time so hard that he yelped. And then she impulsively stepped forward—and bumped squarely into the car. Reaching out to feel the shape in front of her, she immediately realized what had happened. Dropping to her knees, she threw her arms around her dog, and spoke sobbing words into his ear. I couldn't hear what she said, but my guess is that she was admitting how wrong she was, begging for his forgiveness, and praising him for his faithfulness even when she had treated him so badly.

When Peace Doesn't Come Easily

Peacemaking doesn't always turn out the way we want it to. Sometimes we strive for peace without reaching the success we hoped for. We might do everything according to a good plan without getting good results. Although some opponents readily make peace, others stubbornly and defensively resist our efforts to reconcile. Sometimes they grow more antagonistic and even go hunting for new ways to frustrate or mistreat us. At times we encounter negative responses to our peacemaking efforts that are utterly incomprehensible!

When we can't resolve conflict, we face an enormous temptation to take matters into our own hands. We think, "God's way didn't work, so it must be time to try a new approach." One natural reaction is to back away from a relationship and stop doing any kind of good to our opponent. Another is to strike back at people who resist us. Without determined effort, we inevitably fall back into escaping or attacking, the same sinful responses we have worked so hard to be free from.

God doesn't want us to give up on peace or get tangled up fighting the way the world does. This isn't the time to "close the Bible" on a problem, but rather to dig deeper into Scripture. Our goal isn't to beat down or destroy our opponents, but to win them over, help them see the truth, and bring them into a right relationship with God.

In most people's eyes this approach seems naïve. But God offers us a fresh and hopeful way of dealing with even the most intractable conflicts. The apostle Paul knew this. He had learned that God's ways aren't the world's ways. He writes, "For though we live in the world, we do not wage war as the world does. The weapons we fight with are not the weapons of the world" (2 Corinthians 10:3–4). We are to wage a spiritual war using spiritual weapons given to us by God. So how do we proceed? Scripture tells us how.

Pray for Your Enemies

When we stall in our attempts to resolve a conflict, the first thing we can do is to pray again. By now we know that every conflict is too big for us to solve on our own. But conflicts that stretch on and seem unsolvable are noisy reminders that all our efforts depend on God. Only God changes hearts. Prayer is our opportunity to focus on God and recommit ourselves to following his ways. Jesus taught, "Love your enemies, do good to those who hate you, bless those who curse you, pray for those who mistreat you" (Luke 6:27–28). When we face stubborn conflicts, Jesus calls us to pray.

> Prayer is our opportunity to **focus on** God and **recommit** ourselves to his ways.

Guard Your Heart and Your Tongue

As conflict lingers, it's crucial to guard our hearts. What does that mean? Paul wrote, "Bless those who persecute you, bless and do not curse" (Romans 12:14). When you "bless and do not curse," you strive to maintain a right heart attitude toward your opponent. That's a commitment you made when you promised to extend heart forgiveness to your enemy even before reconciliation takes place. Maintaining this disposition not only leaves the door open for reconciliation, but also protects you against bitterness. And it enables you to think much more wisely and constructively than you would if you let your heart dwell on its hurt.

The state of your heart is usually reflected in the words coming from your mouth. The more intense a dispute becomes, the more important it is to control your tongue. When you face prolonged conflict, you might be worn down by temptations to give in to gossip, slander, and reckless words, especially if your opponent is saying critical things about you. Yet if you give in to harsh words, you make matters worse. So make every effort to say only what is both true and helpful, speaking well of your opponent whenever possible, using the kindest language you know. As Peter wrote, "Do not repay evil with evil or insult with insult, but with blessing, because to this you were called so that you may inherit a blessing" (1 Peter 3:9).

Seek Godly Advice

Because it's so difficult to battle evil alone, we need support from people who encourage us and give us biblically sound counsel. Christians are surrounded by advice that doesn't measure up to God's standards. We're constantly coached to fight back, stand up for our rights, or drag our opponents to court. When conflict stretches on, it's tempting not only to give ear to this kind of advice but to seek it out—for example, in difficult marriages heading toward divorce. Yet Proverbs 13:20 says, "He who walks with the wise grows wise, but a companion of fools suffers harm."

Godly advisors are especially helpful when you're involved in a tough conflict and aren't seeing the results you want. If a lack of noticeable progress causes you to doubt the biblical principles you're trying to follow, you might be tempted to abandon God's ways and resort to the tactics you see others using all around you. Seek out friends who encourage you to stay the course, endure under trial, and prioritize obeying God over all else. Make sure you let people into your life who are willing to correct when they see you doing wrong.

Keep Doing Right

The Bible emphasizes the importance of continuing to do right even when it seems that an opponent will never cooperate. Romans 12:17 says, "Do not repay anyone evil for evil. Be careful to do what is right in the eyes of everybody." Being careful to do what is right "in the eyes of everybody" doesn't mean we should be slaves to others' opinions. The Greek word translated *be careful* means "to give thought to the future," "to plan in advance," or "to take careful precaution." Therefore, what Paul is saying is that you should plan and act so carefully and so properly that any reasonable person watching you will eventually acknowledge that what you did was right. Peter taught the same principle when he wrote, "Live such good lives among the pagans that, though they accuse you of doing wrong, they may see your good deeds and glorify God on the day he visits us" (1 Peter 2:12). Even if other people don't choose to do right, your decision to keep doing right honors God.

> Even if other people don't choose to do right, your decision to keep doing right honors God.

Recognize Your Limits

As you deal with difficult people, it's crucial to recognize your limits. Even when you continue to do right, some people will adamantly refuse to live at peace with you. Opponents might keep treating you unkindly, angrily, unfairly, or harshly. And so the Bible makes clear that peace doesn't completely depend on you. It truly takes two to make peace. Paul wrote, "If it is possible, as far as it depends on you, live at peace with everyone" (Romans 12:18). In other words, do everything you can to be reconciled to others, but remember that you can't force others to do good. If you have done everything within your power to resolve a conflict, then you have fulfilled your responsibility. If circumstances change and you have new opportunities to actively seek peace with an opponent, seize those moments. But in the meantime, don't make your whole life revolve around achieving immediate reconciliation.

It's easier to accept your limits if you have a biblical view of success. Most people define success in terms of what someone possesses, controls, or accomplishes. But God defines success in terms of faithful obedience to his commands. The world wants to know, "What results have you achieved?" God asks, "Were you faithful to my ways?" The Lord controls the ultimate outcome of all you do. Therefore, he knows that even your best efforts won't always accomplish the results you want. This is why he doesn't hold you accountable for specific results. Instead, he asks for only one thing—obedience to what he shows you to do. "Fear God and keep his commandments, for this is the whole duty of man" (Ecclesiastes 12:13). If you have made every effort to be reconciled to someone, you have fulfilled your duty. You are a success in God's eyes. Let him take it from there.

Part of recognizing your limits is rejecting the temptation to take revenge on someone who continues to do wrong. God is responsible for doing justice and punishing people who don't repent. Proverbs 20:22 is helpful: "Do not say, 'I'll pay you back for this wrong!' Wait for the Lord, and he will deliver you." Instead of taking matters into your own hands, respect and cooperate with God's methods for dealing with people who persist in doing wrong. Sometimes he uses life circumstances to bring someone around. At times he brings to bear on a person the influence of a larger group, like a business hierarchy or church leadership. In some cases it might be appropriate for you to pursue litigation. Sometimes, however, all you are to do is wait for God to deal with people in his own way. (Psalms 37 and

73 give us a glimpse of how he does this.) Although his results might come more slowly than you want, they will always be better than anything you could bring about on your own.

God's results will always be better than anything you could bring about on your own.

The Ultimate Weapon—Deliberate, Focused Love

When conflict rages on, there is a final tactic to pursue that many think is crazy. We can continue to love our enemy. We use the same weapon God used to win over our hearts. *Love.* Unexpected and undeserved love can break down even the most stubborn heart. Paul describes this principle for responding to an obstinate opponent: " 'If your enemy is hungry, feed him; if he is thirsty, give him something to drink. In doing this, you will heap burning coals on his head.' Do not be overcome by evil, but overcome evil with good" (Romans 12:20–21).

Deliberate, focused love is the ultimate weapon. Instead of reacting spitefully to those who mistreat you, you can discern their deepest needs and do everything you can to meet those needs. Sometimes that means going to them to show them their faults. At other times there may be a need for mercy and compassion, patience, and words of encouragement. You might even discover opportunities to provide material or financial assistance to opponents who least deserve it or expect it from you.

Deliberate, focused love has an irresistible power. Ancient armies often used burning coals to fend off attackers (see Psalm 120:4). No soldier could resist this weapon for long. It eventually overcame even the most determined attacker. Love has the same overwhelming power. At the very least, actively loving an enemy protects you from being spiritually defeated by anger, bitterness, and thirst for revenge. And, in some cases, your active and determined love for your opponent may be used by God to bring that person to repentance.

Just as that Seeing Eye dog continued to do what was good and eventually experienced his owner's repentance, we too can draw on God's grace to overcome evil with good.

Coming Back to the Gospel

While the hope is that our enemy will turn and we will enjoy full reconciliation, this will not always happen, at least not right away. Even so, the gospel of Christ inspires and empowers us to continue doing what is right, regardless of what others do.

As we delight in the gospel, we can replace our desire for self-vindication with a desire to please and honor God. We can put aside the tendency to dwell on others' wrongs and cooperate with God as he helps us repent of our own sins and put on the character of Christ. We can develop the courage and ability to correct others lovingly and effectively, then wait patiently as God works to fulfill his purpose in their lives. We can find joy in offering to others the undeserved forgiveness that we ourselves have received from God through Christ. The gospel is the joy and delight and perfect road map of every true peacemaker!

Let the peace of Christ rule in your hearts,
since as members of one body you were called to peace.
And be thankful.

Colossians 3:15

GOING DEEPER

To dig deeper into what the Bible teaches about peacemaking, read my more detailed book, *The Peacemaker: A Biblical Guide to Resolving Personal Conflict* (Baker Books, 2004). We also have a Web site (*www.Peacemaker.net*) loaded with other resources, true stories, and information about training that equips people to help others resolve conflict of every kind.

APPENDIX

Questions for Reflection and Discussion

The following questions will help you apply what you are learning to your day-to-day life and relationships.

One—The Nature of Conflict

When in a conflict, ask yourself the following types of questions:

1. What have my primary goals been as I have responded to this dispute?

2. What attitudes and desires have I had that made the conflict worse?

3. Was the original cause of this conflict a difference in opinion, a misunderstanding, or someone's sinful attitude or desire?

4. How could I respond to this conflict in a way that shows Jesus' transforming power in my life?

5. How might God be working for my good through this dispute?

Two—The Hope of the Gospel

1. How would you describe the gospel in your own words?

2. Do you believe that Jesus is God's Son and that he came to reconcile you with God? If so, how has this belief changed your heart and life? How has it changed your response to conflict?

If you are presently in a conflict:

3. Where do you seem to be stuck? What do you believe or feel you should do but just don't have the strength to do it?

4. How could focusing on the gospel—how God saved you from the penalty and power of sin through his Son's death—motivate and enable you to deal with this conflict in a constructive way?

Three—Escaping, Attacking, or Peacemaking

1. Do you tend to see conflict as a problem to avoid, an obstacle to conquer, or an opportunity to do good? How does your view impact your response to conflict?

2. Describe a time when you damaged a relationship by either attacking or escaping.

If you are presently in a conflict:

3. Review the Slippery Slope diagram on page 37. Which response have *you* used in this dispute? What has been the result so far?

4. Which response do you believe God is calling you to use at this time? How do you think that response could change the course of this conflict?

Four—G1: Go Higher

1. Do you find it difficult to trust God when you are in conflict? Why?

2. How would your feelings, attitudes, or behavior change if you were able to start seeing conflict as an opportunity to trust, obey, and imitate God?

If you are presently in a conflict:

3. What are some questions, doubts, or fears that you have in your present conflict?

4. If someone has offended you, what are the pros and cons of simply overlooking that offense? Which choice do you think you would be happiest about when you look back on this situation a year from now?

5. Read Psalms 37 and 73. What do these psalms say you *should not do* in this conflict? What do they say you *should do*?

Five—G2: Get Real

1. Why is it so hard for us to admit our part in causing a conflict?

2. Which of the Seven A's do you struggle with the most when you know you need to admit you've been wrong?

If you are presently in a conflict:

3. Can you identify any of your own attitudes, words, or actions that have made the conflict worse? Are any of them sinful?

4. Using the Seven A's as a model, write a confession.

5. How do you want to change as a result of this conflict? Pick out one character quality you wish to grow in and decide on one step you will take to practice that quality.

6. Pray that God would help you see your own sin clearly and confess it honestly and completely.

Six—G3: Gently Engage

1. Do you have any reason to believe that someone else has something against you?

2. Why is it important to initiate a conversation with someone with whom you are in conflict even when you believe it's not your fault?

3. Why is it important to understand that people get "caught" in sin? (See Galatians 6:1.)

If you are presently in a conflict:

4. Is it hard for you to talk to the person who has hurt or offended you? Is it easy? Why?

5. If this offense is too serious to overlook, is it better to go directly to that person yourself, or involve someone else right away?

6. How do you think the other person might respond to you? What should you say—and what should you not say—to make it easier for the other person to listen openly to your concerns?

Seven—G4: Get Together

1. Why is it important to understand how God has forgiven us in order to truly forgive others?

2. Is it possible to forgive when we still feel hurt or angry? Why?

If you are presently in a conflict:

3. How has your opponent sinned against you?

4. Has he or she committed any unconfessed sins that you can overlook and forgive right now?

5. How does the forgiveness you've received through Christ help you to forgive others in this situation?

6. If you decide to forgive, how will you show that you really mean it?

Eight—Overcome Evil with Good

1. Are you ever tempted to just "close your Bible" and give up when people don't respond well in conflict?

2. How can the gospel of Jesus Christ guide, motivate, and empower you when the going gets rough?

If you are presently in a conflict:

3. To whom can you turn for godly advice and encouragement?

4. What can you keep on doing that is "right" in your conflict situation?

5. What needs does your opponent have that God may want you to meet? In other words, how can you actively and deliberately love your opponent?

ABOUT THE AUTHORS

Ken Sande, founder of Peacemaker Ministries (*www.Peacemaker.net*), is passionate about bringing the life-changing power of God's peacemaking principles to people around the world.

Ken has spoken on six continents and has ministered to parties in hundreds of conflicts, ranging from simple personal issues to complex disputes. His book *The Peacemaker: A Biblical Guide to Resolving Personal Conflict* has been translated into a dozen languages. He coauthored a book for teens, *The Peacemaker Student Edition*, and one on family relationships, *Peacemaking for Families*.

Ken is a history buff who loves to run. The Sande family enjoys hiking and cross-country skiing in the mountains near their home in Montana.

Kevin Johnson is the bestselling author or coauthor of more than fifty books and Bible products for kids, youth, and adults. As the former senior editor at Bethany House Publishers, Kevin oversaw a major adult nonfiction line.

Kevin currently serves as Pastor of Emmaus Road Church in Minneapolis. His training includes an MDiv from Fuller Theological Seminary and a BA in English and Print Journalism from the University of Wisconsin—River Falls.

Kevin's interests include trail running, cycling, radio (with broadcasts heard on AM and shortwave), and digital photography. Kevin lives with his wife, Lyn, their three children, several dozen tropical fish, and a champion blue merle Sheltie named Channisce. Learn more at *kevinjohnsonbooks.com*.

ACKNOWLEDGMENTS

To the Board of Directors of Peacemaker Ministries—
Alfred, Don, Jim, Julius, Karen, Manfred, Mark, Oletha,
Ruth, Tom, and Tom—who have guided our ministry so faith-
fully over the years and inspired us to serve people from every
walk of life, all around the world.

Know anyone else who's tired of
FIGHTING?

Resolving Everyday Conflict is also available as an eight-week DVD study for groups.

This dynamic video series unpacks the amazing things the Bible says about conflict and relationships in a fun and non-threatening manner. It includes practical teaching, engaging video case studies, group discussion activities, devotions during the week to engrain the lessons, and materials to help you implement the study in a church or workplace setting.

*Also available in an **online e-learning format** for self-study or for groups with difficulty getting together in one location.*

For more information, visit www.Peacemaker.net/REC

Peacemaker Ministries

Bringing real answers to broken relationships

Much more practical help on living reconciled
relationships at home, at work, and in your church
is available through Peacemaker Ministries.

Resources • Training • Conflict Assistance

Visit **www.Peacemaker.net** for more information.

"'Blessed are the peacemakers,' said Jesus. With crystal clarity this manual lays before us the wisdom that leads humble souls into that blessing."

—J. I. Packer, author of *Knowing God*

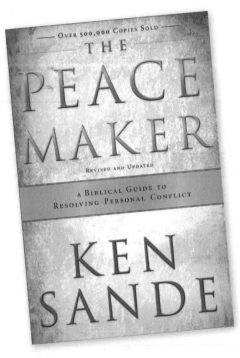

In *The Peacemaker*, Ken Sande presents practical biblical guidance for conflict resolution that takes you beyond resolving conflicts to true, life-changing reconciliation with family, coworkers, and fellow believers.

BakerBooks
a division of Baker Publishing Group
www.BakerBooks.com

Available wherever books and ebooks are sold.

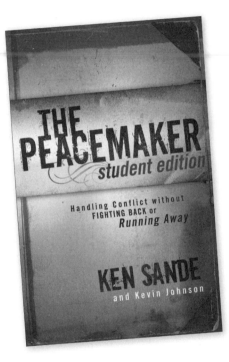

"Make every effort to keep the unity of the Spirit through the bond of peace."–Ephesians 4:3

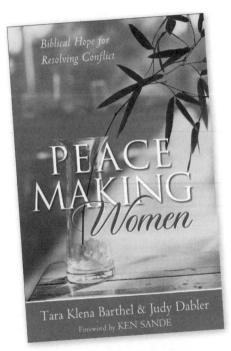

Peacemaking Women offers a meaningful, lasting message to lead you out of conflict and into a state of peace where you can live as a representative of Christ to other women as well as to unbelievers. With personal stories and advice that is firmly rooted in Scripture, the authors guide you to peace with God, peaceful relationships with others, and genuine peace within.

PEACEMAKING:
The healing alternative to conflict in the church

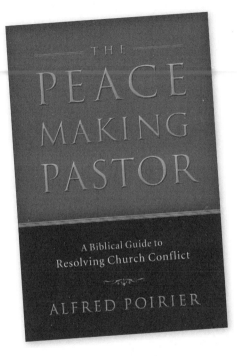

With this comprehensive guide, you can embrace peacemaking confidently as a way to glorify God through the overcoming power of the gospel. And, as Jesus promised all peacemakers, you will be blessed.